PRAISE

Confessions from the Heart [illegible] *oach*

"Dan Foxx has been my coach for fifteen years spanning three companies and is always 'in my corner.' His passion for making a difference in people's lives has been amazing, and he has consistently been successful with me and my executive teams. His book is a must-read for anyone trying to make a difference in their own lives."

—Dave Zabrowski
CEO, DataCore Software, Inc.
Ft. Lauderdale, FL

"A timeless trove of semi-recent Silicon Valley history, life lessons learned, and spiritual insight. Because Dan truly loves his work and his fellow man, he can pass along to us the reasons for success and failure that both hinder and help managers in their careers like few others can. If you are in a career or a life that is not going as you'd like, Dan's book is a true masterpiece at raising awareness of what propels us and prevents us from achieving what we truly want. This is a book that I'll buy and pass on to others whom I really care about when mentoring on how to get what you want in life, love, and happiness."

—Wes Brewer
CEO, ProGrade Digital, Inc.
San Jose, CA

"This book, like its author Dan Foxx, is energetic, authentic, and on the field right where leaders play. The stories and case studies are sure to resonate with leaders looking to form impactful relationships with everyone they work with! Part business, part self-leadership, but wholly about the personal journey that delivers business success. Dan's book makes you feel he's right in the room with you coaching you to win."

—Daniel A. Chen
Head of Business Development, Quicken, Inc.
Menlo Park, CA

"I had the good fortune of meeting Dan in the early 2000s during the start of my CEO career. He is a very passionate coach who greatly influenced my approach to leadership. He helped me to dig deep down inside to identify what I am truly passionate about and using that passion to motivate my team."

—Tom Waechter
Retired CEO, JDS Uniphase
Pleasanton, CA

"As a past executive coaching client of Dan's, I thoroughly enjoyed reading *Confessions from the Heart of an Executive Coach.* The book is an outstanding encapsulation of his unique approach to executive coaching and achieving success both in business and in life. Dan takes us on a deeply personal journey into ourselves, where he so aptly points out how love and the human connection are foundational to our success. He highlights the importance of authenticity, personal passion, commitment, selflessness, and humility in our lives. I highly recommend this reading to anyone interested in acquiring and applying the wisdom of one of the very best executive coaches in the business and one of the finest human beings on the planet."

—Bart Freedman
CEO, Barlen Associates
Portland, OR

"Dan worked with me and my management team during a key period when the company was undergoing a drastic change in product strategy. He's different—very different. If you are truly open to learning some radical things about leadership, and changing the way you think, read this book!"

—John Harte
Former CEO, NeoVista Software
San Francisco Bay Area

"Dan Foxx has been my coach for over a decade. Dan has a unique ability to help his clients capture the essence of a matter—and to help us see through our blind spots. Dan's latest work on the importance of relationship and human connectivity is incredibly powerful because it reminds us what matters most—our relationships with God and our loved ones as the core reason we do what we do. Dan has spoken to groups I have led and is always incredibly inspiring to everyone there. Having Dan as a coach and facilitator is a massive accelerator."

—Brent Dusing
Managing Partner, Gideon Ventures
Founder, Cellfire, Lightside
Austin, TX

CONFESSIONS *from* *the* HEART *of an* EXECUTIVE COACH

TRUE STORIES BEHIND CLOSED DOORS

Why Some CEOs Win Big, While Others Crash and Burn

DAN FOXX

CEO, Unlock Your Leadership

UNLOCK YOUR LEADERSHIP

Confessions from the Heart of an Executive Coach

All the stories are true, but in some cases, to preserve client confidentiality, names have been changed, but no characters are invented, no events fabricated. This book is designed to provide information and inspiration to readers. It is sold with the understanding that the publisher and author are not engaged to render any type of psychological, legal, or any other kind of professional advice. The content is the sole expression and opinion of the author. No warranties or guarantees are expressed or implied by the publisher's choice to include any of the content in this volume. Neither the publisher nor the individual author shall be liable for any physical, psychological, emotional, financial, or commercial damages, including, but not limited to, special, incidental, consequential, or other damages. If emotional issues arise during your reading of this book, seek professional care.

ISBN (paperback): 978-1-7340712-0-7
ISBN (ebook): 978-1-7340712-1-4
ISBN (audiobook): 978-1-7340712-2-1

Book design by www.DominiDragoone.com
Editorial services by Sandra Wendel, Write On, Inc.
Cover photo by Joy Porter

Published by
Unlock Your Leadership

UNLOCK YOUR
LEADERSHIP

Contact the author at:
DanFoxx@UnlockYourLeadership.com
www.UnlockYourLeadership.com

DEDICATION

This book is sincerely dedicated to God who has caressed me through the many deep trials of my life and through them rendered humility, grace, and wisdom. Who blessed me with the opportunity to spend over 50,000 hours of intimate one-on-one time with over 4,500 executives during the last twenty-two years. Who gave me the gift of a spectacular calling that fits like a glove and has rendered a very profitable profession.

I also dedicate this book to the thousands of executives who opened their hearts and minds to me. Who revealed their most intimate emotions and secrets. Who were vulnerable with me and let me share in their pain and victories. To those clients who helped me to grow as a man and a coach by watching their courage to take themselves on in an honest and powerful way.

CONTENTS

1

WHEN YOUR LIFE FITS LIKE A GLOVE

When a major piece of the puzzle of your life falls into place, it usually comes from personal epiphanies—breakthrough insights of brilliance and hard work over an extended period of time. It's times like these when you just know the planets are aligned. What you are doing and who you are fit like a glove. This feeling is often a surprise, always a gift. As if your whole life is a treasure map with a clear X over the buried gold.

It was late summer of 1997. I had just opened my executive coaching practice. I probably had three CEOs as clients at that time. One weekend I was in South Shore, Lake Tahoe walking around an outdoor festival replete with candles, artwork, essential oils, and kettle corn. The environment was ideal for people watching.

As I was wandering about, I saw someone who startled me. I couldn't believe my eyes. Dr. Leo Buscaglia. I recognized him from his photo on the back of his books I had read, and from his extensive interviews on television.

Dr. Buscaglia was a professor at USC. He had written fourteen books. Five of them were on the *New York Times* best-seller list at the same time. In my heart I always thought of him as a rock star when it came to love, relationships, human transformation, and connection. Something about his work was incredibly special to me. It seemed to be his ability to reach through the pages or the television screen and authentically transmit his emotion to the point that I was moved. He was charismatic, naturally inspiring to listen to, and completely authentic in who he was as a man and what he stood for in the world.

Looking back at that day, I clearly see what it was that I respected so: his pure and complete love for people. When you listened to or read Leo, you could tell he was holding nothing back, and you just knew he was talking directly to you.

Maybe three seconds after I recognized him, I moved in for the meet. His back was to me when I said, "Dr. Buscaglia, my name is Dan Foxx." As he turned to face me, my hand was already extended toward him. A big and genuine smile lit his face and, without hesitation, ignoring my outstretched hand, he raised both arms, took one step toward me, and gave me a full embrace hug. It wasn't one of those halfhearted "bro" hugs with one arm and a pat on the back. No, it was a full, arms around me, tight hug, with much of our torsos touching.

As he encompassed me, he lowered his head warmly into the pocket of my neck. It was the kind of hug a proud dad would give a service-member son at the airport when returning from a war.

The Hug, as I now refer to it, lasted a good three seconds. As he pulled away, his hands gently slid down my arms to each elbow, where he gently retained a light grip.

Staring deeply into my eyes, he said the craziest thing. "Dan, it's so great to finally meet you." He said it with compassion and authentic meaning.

I instantaneously knew it was his truth. But I couldn't understand how he meant it. Now please realize he didn't know me from Adam. I was no one in his world. But I felt, in the depths of my soul, that he completely meant what he just said. I was aghast and unprepared for that. We were not ten seconds into our meeting each other, and I knew he loved me. And I had no idea why.

It felt like he was saying, "Oh, my goodness, where have you been? Here, let me take a look at you." It genuinely felt like home, as if

Norman Rockwell had painted the moment. His eyes were completely fixed on mine. I think a bomb could have gone off nearby, and he wouldn't have noticed.

For the next few minutes, no one else existed in the world to him but me. I noticed that a small group of people, maybe twenty, were starting to circle us, because they recognized him too. But he was oblivious to their presence. He asked me what I did in the world. I told him that I had just started an executive coaching business. He then asked me, "And how's that going?"

I spoke 90 percent of the time, while he just occasionally asked me a clarifying question. He had no interest in himself. There was no one in the world but me in those ten minutes.

He asked me how the coaching business was going, and I told him I was struggling a bit with one aspect of my work.

"My clients will tell me about an issue they're facing and ask for my help. I will offer my advice and my coaching, which I know will work as a solution. But they often respond with something like, 'Well, Dan, I hear what you are saying, but I would argue that, with what these VPs are getting paid, they ought to be mature enough to get along.'"

With compassion in his eyes, he nodded in the affirmative and quietly said, "Ahhh, yes. Dan, you first have to show them the need."

That was it. Nothing more. I had no idea what that meant, but I knew it was the powerful answer I was looking for. In my awestruck moment, I didn't dare tell him I didn't understand. Heck, I was an enlightened executive coach. But I wanted him to think that I thought his advice was powerful, so I nodded like I completely understood, and thanked him.

In that moment he was Master and I was Grasshopper, or he was Yoda and I was Luke Skywalker. But I knew I would figure out what he said if given a few moments to process. I memorized his advice: "Dan, you first have to show them the need. You first have to show them the need."

We chatted for a couple of more moments and got ready to go our separate ways. As our conversation came to an end, he reached out and hugged me again. With a genuine smile on his face he thanked me for introducing myself to him. I didn't want to move. I didn't want the meeting to end, but I knew it must. I wanted to spend two whole days with him, but I was enormously grateful for that ten minutes.

I have never experienced such complete love and acceptance from anyone in my entire life. I truly felt that he was excitedly happy to finally get to meet *me*. He made me feel like I had just made his day. For those ten minutes, no one else mattered and nothing else existed in Leo's life but me. But it was the hug that changed my life. There is a dopamine hit that our body produces with human contact, and when you couple loving words with the hug, the combination is incredibly powerful.

PUT THE PIECES TOGETHER

As I drove the three and a half hours back home to the Bay Area, I was rolling his words over and over in my mind. "Dan, you first have to show them the need. You first have to show them the need." What did that mean? Uhhhh. I had no clue. I broke that one sentence down.

Dan, you "*first*—" Okay, before anything else first. "*Have to*—" It's not an option. It's a necessity. "*Show*—" So it's not speaking, training, coaching, telling, teaching, or advising, it's showing. For something to be shown, it would have to be a quality already present inside me in order for it to be naturally revealed or shown to others. It would have to be something that just emanates outwardly from my eyes and the pores of my skin. I can't show something I don't already have.

And then "*the need*." What is the need? It must be something they don't have, maybe something they don't even know they don't have, or maybe something they don't even know they should want. What is their common need? All my clients are so different, so the need would have to be really basic, like at the core of human desire. It would have to be something that is not tied to the diversity of their personalities.

I made a list: They all want success. But why? Because they want to be respected? They want to give money to others, like their spouses and children, mom and dad?

Maybe they think that their success would cause them to be better loved and more respected. Heck, I didn't know what each of these diverse people wants that is common to all of them.

I wrote a list based on my experience so far.

Clients want people to want to follow their leadership, which means, as leaders, they want to help their team and be loved for the helping. But I realized that is not necessarily so. Some CEOs deploy commander authority and threats to get obedience, so they don't care about being liked.

Maybe their common need is to matter in their world.

Maybe they all want to be accepted, appreciated, and loved.

Maybe they want to feel that they are enough.

I got a little tired trying to unravel the riddle, and my mind began to wander. It gravitated back to the hug and Leo's genuine smile—eyes fixed on mine. My heart warmed all over again when I reflected on my meeting, and I thought, boy, I *needed* that hug. Then it hit me. I just spoke the word *needed*. I had this instantaneous, bold epiphany. I needed to be loved and accepted for exactly who I am. And while I was with Leo, I was. And that is the primal need for every one of my clients.

It's a primal/basic need for every one of us to be loved and accepted. No one wants to admit it, but that's what we all really want and have always wanted. Some think that success and money will bring love and acceptance, but they don't realize that's a fool's errand. Because one of the downsides of success is the response of friends. Some friends will abandon you because you are successful. The friends can become jealous, or they just assume you won't have the time for them anymore. The successful person's friends want to matter in this world, too, and they want to matter to you.

And then it hit me again. I thought my mind was going to explode. His advice to me was exactly what he exemplified and showed to me during our meeting. He was doing exactly what he was telling me to do. When he looked at me, he was thinking, "Leo, you first, have to, show Dan, the need." He showed me the need I didn't recognize that I deeply wanted. He knew that I, like everyone else, desperately needed to be loved and accepted, and he wanted me to experience the lesson he was showing me.

He didn't teach. He *was* the expression of love, and I got it in spades. He was his advice to me. And I didn't need success or riches that afternoon. I had respect, love, acceptance, and his undivided attention. All what I thought success would provide, I received in that ten minutes. I mattered in those moments to someone I didn't even know, and I needed nothing else to feel complete.

As I look back on that sunny afternoon, I feel so grateful for that providential meeting. Sadly, Leo passed away just a few short months after our meeting at the festival in that casino parking lot in Lake Tahoe. But I am left with profound gratitude for the gift and blessing of meeting him before he moved on from this earth. Even today, I feel like the luckiest man in the world. Even today, all over again, as I write this story, I am deeply moved.

That afternoon, I got something like eight college semesters of valuable breakthrough emotional quotient training in ten minutes. Not only that, I was addicted to what I had learned. I was now on a mission.

THE BIG BUSINESS TRANSFORMATION

Thanks to Leo's hug, I stopped entering my clients' offices to help them with their problems. I wasn't there to advise them or give them my opinion. I was there to love them and make sure they knew they were enough, and that they were completely accepted by me. My goal was to make sure that I was truly glad to see them. Then, and only then, would I offer my coaching. And then, and only then, I would find that they would seek my guidance and take it into their lives.

I don't know who the original author of this quote is, but I love it. "People don't care how much you know until they know how much you care." Yes, the pieces of the puzzle Leo gave me all fell into place.

Now I needed to discover how to authentically love my clients before starting each coaching session. This became even more challenging when I was meeting a client for the first time. How was I going to love someone I had never met? How did Leo do it? I created my own solution.

I pictured each client as a four-year-old child. I imagined that all this child wanted was to have fun and be loved and accepted. I pictured them in my heart and mind as having no evil thoughts and doing no evil deeds. They were all too young and innocent. I then pictured all the kinds of feelings they must have felt over the years since growing up. I know they must have felt

- Loving,
- Fearful,
- Proud,
- Betrayed,
- Jealous,
- Excited,
- Sad,
- Disappointed,
- Rejected,
- Jubilant,
- Passionate,
- Longing,
- Victorious,
- Frustrated,
- Compassionate,
- Giving,
- Resentful, and more.

I realized that I already knew my clients intimately because I, too, have felt the same feelings. Now, I don't know which feeling they are experiencing at a particular moment, but regardless of what emotion they are feeling, I have felt it also. I don't know the stories of what happened to make them feel each emotion, but I could find out.

The main point was not the events that caused the emotions; it was the emotions themselves that we have in common. I have felt every emotion they have felt. I completely knew everyone I met because we have shared exactly the same feelings over our lifetimes. This empowered me to enter every meeting with a deep love for my clients. I could genuinely say, as Leo did to me, "It's so great to finally meet you."

My coaching business exploded overnight.

Within the span of one year I was coaching thirty-one CEOs each month. That was a tenfold increase in business in twelve months. Executive team offsites had to be held on Saturdays, because I was swamped during the week with one-on-one coaching sessions. There was a time I was charging $5,800 per session, and each session lasted only an hour and a half. Executive team offsites were billed at $20,000. I was flying all over the country. Eventually I coached in Amsterdam, Paris, and Mumbai. But I recall that all this was ignited because of a ten-minute experience with Leo Buscaglia. True transformation can occur in just moments. Leo's hug truly changed my life.

My business transformation came because I discovered how to love my clients. They understood that I wasn't there for the money, or to tell them what to do. I accepted them for exactly who they were and where they were. This allowed them to be vulnerable, to tell me authentically what was on their heart.

After years of studying this concept, I have found that vulnerability is in fact highly contagious. Have you ever told someone something that required deep vulnerability on your part, only to find that, after they listened, they told you something really sensitive about their lives? My clients have told me stuff about their lives that I knew they never told anyone, even their spouse. It was uncomfortable for them, but they did it. Many of my clients over the years have become dear friends. I have since realized that this statement, attributed to various others through the years, remains true: "People don't care how much you know until they know how much you care."

If you love all the people in your life, they will risk being honest and vulnerable in return. They will trust you when you love them and be willing to love you back. They will do this because they know you care first about them. Without love, they feel like a pawn, a thing to be moved about on the chessboard of life so you can reach your own end game.

When you get off yourself and your self-centered thoughts and just focus your attention on loving others, everything, with a little time, will just fall into place. Getting off yourself and completely focusing on others is the most important part of our work together in the coming chapters.

TAKEAWAYS

- Dr. Leo Buscaglia perfectly modeled the principles in this chapter. He was completely unselfish, came from love, and focused on me. This instantly created deep human connection between us.
- Human connection creates willing listeners, engenders trust, and moves the human heart.
- Something powerful, beyond our understanding, happens when we are loved and accepted for who we are without any judgment.

- This kind of instantaneous connection that can be created can change people's lives forever.
- We can love others even before we meet them, because we know all the emotions they have felt. The same ones you have experienced. This can create empathy and understanding. It is through this connection that we can come to love the next person we meet, before we meet them.
- It is this kind of human connection and caring that shows up in your career as causing massive success.
- The key is to be so okay with yourself that you can focus on others first.

2

THE PROMISE

Let's get into the meat of how success works and reengineer or deconstruct how to get there.

Almost everything you have probably learned about success may be a contributor to the quest for success, but what you learned misses the mark completely about the foundation that creates success. A fundamental spark ignites the inferno of massive success that almost all academic training completely misses. That foundation is the human heart. With that in mind, I promise to empower you here in these words to show you how and to ignite that spark in the human heart to create success in your business and personal life. Period.

Some of the principles I offer you are as old as humanity walking the face of the earth but explored in a new way, while others will be new to you. Written here are the tools for you to ignite success in relationships, which you will discover is the first necessary step toward success everywhere—at home and in the workplace.

The dilemma is that while we think we know the principles of success, often we are way off base. If what we were previously taught was all we needed, then we would all be massively successful already today. My job is to reveal to you these principles, through real stories of CEOs and VPs—clients that I have worked with over the past twenty-two years. It is my deep desire that, through the stories of my work with them, you discover your blind spots and begin to see success in a totally new light.

If you are willing to set aside your previous learning and beliefs of yourself and your world, then you will want to shift your belief system. It is your belief system that drives your attitudes, words, and actions to deploy this power into your life. This is not a "what to do and how to do it" book. This is a book about introspection, personal shifting of beliefs, and growth, so you show up as a more whole and complete person—who happens to also make a great leader.

You really can have a spectacular life. One that is fulfilling, successful, and full of joy. Yes, *you*. It's okay if you have already dropped any previously held aspirations of a grand and fulfilling life. We can pick up from right where you are and change your trajectory. It's sad that today positive affirmations are little more than empty platitudes or just sayings on a motivational poster in the breakroom.

But here is why my promise is different: I am personally committed to you. Starting right here and now, I desperately want you to live fully, whole, and complete. And I know you can succeed at a life much bigger and bolder than what you may be experiencing now. I am just asking you to believe, just a bit, that what I am promising is true—for you. And keep reading.

I want you to be the author of your life, not just a reporter covering the story of your life. I want you to play on the field of your life and take bold action to create a life truly worth living.

Now here is where I need you to just trust me for just a bit. I am about to make a crazy statement: I love you. Sounds crazy to read that, I know, because we don't know each other. But I will explain that crazy comment in such a way that you will come to truly believe me.

Now at this point, your ego and self-protection mechanisms are probably screaming, "Yeah, right. Not me. This guy must be all about the soft and squishy stuff. I don't feel like that's possible. What he's said so far is just too good to be true. No one I know lives like that."

But I still mean what I wrote. I don't care about judging your past, or what you consider to be your capabilities. I still believe completely in you and your future, even if you don't. How can I say this? I have worked with over 4,500 people during the last twenty-two years in my work as an executive coach and uncovered and encouraged their brilliant potential, and I will do the same for you.

Look, you have purchased this book, and here we are. All I ask is that you believe in yourself, even if you have to pretend, because I believe in you.

Over the last two decades as an executive coach, I know what it takes to succeed. I'll take you there. But then we are going to dive deeply inside who you are, including your heart, and your beliefs of self and this world, so you can change. You do want to change your outcome in life in some way, right?

It's like a skyscraper in New York. No one wants to talk about the foundation, the rebar, and geology tests of the soil to make the building stand strong. They want to see the skyscraper already up and watch the flag pole triumphantly mounted on the top. Fair enough. We'll start with massive success and take the elevator down to bedrock upon which we will build the necessary foundation to make your skyscraper or, in this context, your success and your life, grow with stability and structural integrity. By the time we get to the foundation, you will be fascinated with reengineering the inner workings of your heart and mind.

When I am coaching a client. I listen carefully to what is bothering them. And, yes, right away we tackle the immediate issues with solutions, strategies, and tactics. But once that is accomplished, we go deeper. I want to know what dynamics were in place that allowed the issue to arise in the first place. Often it's their leadership, which is the result of who they are as humans.

Your leadership is the manifestation of who you are. Deeper still are the personal issues that led to the scenario even occurring under your watch, not to mention the wounds that initiated the personal issues that often continue to haunt you. Solve those underlying issues and you are on your way to better leadership and more integrated and effortless success as a wholehearted leader.

Follow this train of thought down to the bedrock:

- Your success—your search for peace, success, joy, fulfillment, and contribution—is a direct result of the quality and investment you make in all your relationships. Success, a promotion, or growing sales are all predicated on your relationships. Adventure and peace will come from the relationships with your peers and direct reports. Happiness and joy are rooted in your relationships with your family and friends.
- Life and leadership success is all about relationships.
- Relationships are dependent on your ability to "get off yourself" and make an emotional investment in others, through love and vulnerability.
- Love and vulnerability will require that you overcome your fear of how you are seen by others. This will involve facing your fear and putting yourself at risk to make these investments.
- In order to overcome your fear, you will first really get to know yourself and become grounded. This confrontation will enable you to love yourself with healthy self-love and solid self-esteem.
- Knowing and loving yourself will require you to become reconciled with your past, so you become free from the negative influences of wounds and resentments. It's this past emotional baggage that has caused you to be exactly where you are today.
- These principles are tough to address, but your future is at stake. Is it worth it? Hell yes. Is it easy? Hell no. But realize that if nothing changes, then nothing changes.

To summarize these bullets, when you are free from your past wounds, resentments, and self-protection mechanisms, you can then feel a sense of love for others. Through this love you will find yourself able to show up as vulnerable to people, which is attractive because you're now authentic. It is through your ability to express vulnerability that you will find the keys to open the doors to everything you want in your life, like mammoth, meaningful relationships. If you want success, what you need is empowered relationships.

You will come to see that relationships are your life. Take a moment and see for yourself. I say that your life consists of spouse or partner, children, friends, the people in your church, golf or fishing buddies, boss, peers and direct reports, and even the lady at the cash register at the last store you visited. Each one contributes to your life through relationships. The goal is to empower all these relationships to work for you, not against you. I am not being slimy here, like manipulating them in some way. I am saying that the way we make relationships work for us is to contribute unconditionally out of love for them first.

Your success is an inside job. Success in the material and emotional world starts with you, your heart, beliefs, and thoughts. Success is a place we come from, not a place that we get to. When we come from an authentic, loving place in our hearts, and because we are free from the anchor of past emotional wounds and resentments, we are a magnet to all people. They will want to come alongside us and be with us, and just naturally want to help us win. Conflict mostly goes away. And whatever remains doesn't really matter to you anymore, because you are so grounded in who you are that no one can mess with you. I call this state being *un-messable.*

How many thousands of emotional traumas have occurred in your life? Instead of being shared, processed, and let go of, they were buried and affected how you showed up in the world.

It is critical to authentically know yourself. But this insight requires that we need to be courageous enough to look behind the scenes and see what we are feeling and discover why those feelings are there. Only then can we choose to act, or react, on purpose.

When I have a wound or resentment, it causes me to not like myself. When you are clean from the emotional baggage of the past, you will fall in love with you. I mean that in the most humble way. You finally get to become your own best friend. You can actually like spending time with yourself; nothing needs to be added for you to feel whole and complete.

It was that kind of moment for me when I experienced the intense love and acceptance of Dr. Leo Buscaglia. During our ten-minute spontaneous huddle, Leo was moved and inspired, and so was I. In those moments in the parking lot of a festival, nothing needed to be added to make us feel quenched.

TAKEAWAYS

- Here, I am giving you a macro blueprint of this work.
- You must believe in yourself. Believe in your dreams. If that's not possible at this moment, please at least trust that I believe in you. I have gone deep with over 4,500 people. That experience has taught me to authentically believe in the human potential. That potential is you. Let that be enough for now.
- If you are human, and I know you are, and you are older than eighteen, then you have emotional wounds. They will need to be addressed a little later to find the freedom and belief in yourself. Especially your belief that you can and deserve to win at life.
- Everything you want in life will come from your relationships. Relationships are built when we are able to get off of our self-centeredness and focus on others.

3

GO AFTER WHAT YOU WANT

I was nineteen years old, 240 miles from home, driving up a busy boulevard in Walnut Creek, California. As I squinted at my *Thomas Guide*, I questioned why I ever allowed my friend Bob Edmondson to talk me into paying for and going to a motivational seminar.

When I got my real estate license at eighteen years old, Bob was my real estate broker. I listened to him and became inspired by what he told me. He said he saw real potential in me. Since Bob was very successful, and a friend, I almost always followed his advice.

In 1973 motivational seminars were still cool. Yet I was a country boy in the big city, clearly out of my element. I agreed to go because Bob was the first person in the world who authentically believed in me as a man. He believed in my potential, and he proclaimed that I had a bright future. I had never experienced another family member or friend who was so completely in my corner. His belief in me meant a lot; it felt fantastic. Based on his faith in me, I signed up for the seminar.

I found the hotel just in time. Walking into the ballroom, I didn't recognize a soul among the 400 attendees. I was also clearly the youngest person, and my attire was embarrassingly outclassed. I am now embarrassed to say it, but since it was 1973, I was probably wearing a light blue polyester leisure suit, while everyone else in the room was attired in a Hart Schaffner Marx blended wool, three-piece suit. At that point, I was really questioning my decision to attend. But I hung in there.

The first speaker was John Fleur. He was okay. The second speaker was Zig Ziglar, and his words began to stir my heart. But the third speaker, Cavett Robert, ignited a passion in my heart that boiled over. I felt he was speaking directly to me. I hung on his every word. The longer I listened, the more my excitement grew. I can't remember anything in particular he said that day, but I do remember that he exuded an authentic and complete belief in the possibility of who I could become. He expressed absolute certainty that I could succeed at anything I pursued. His message was life-changing.

By the end of Robert's talk, I was all in. I was committed to achieving something grand. Yet I was lost as to what that might be. I was full of passion, ready for success, but had no idea what success looked like. I wanted to change the world, at least my world. I was so moved while he was speaking, it was hard to sit still. I don't know if I have ever felt that kind of intense stirring since.

At the end of the conference I joined the line of attendees who wanted to meet Cavett Robert and shake his hand. When it was finally my turn, I said, "Mr. Robert, it is so great to meet you. That was a fantastic speech. It must be so rewarding to know you are making such a big difference in all these people's lives."

His response shocked me. "Thank you, Dan. But the truth of the matter is that by tracking the attendees' success following a conference we discovered that only 3 percent of the attendees' lives are positively changed by this work."

"No way," I blurted. "How can you be so inspiring knowing that only 3 percent will benefit from what you say?"

He gently smiled and told me that 3 percent is enough. "As a speaker, I am trained to look to the left, center, and right so it looks like I am visually addressing the whole audience. But I try to pick out one person on the left, one in the center, and one on the right and tell myself that these individuals are the 3 percent. I am actually speaking to just three people, but at 50 to 100 feet away it looks like I am speaking to every person in the room."

As I drove home, I made a decision to be in the 3 percent because now I was afraid I would fall into the 97 percent unless I did something different than most of the audience members. As I look back now, his words about reaching 3 percent, while true, were actually intended to make me double down on my commitment. It was a brilliant move. He inspired me into taking bold and consistent action to be in the 3 percent. The conference inspired me to read books—a lot of books. I wanted to feed the steam I had built up during that talk.

One book I read shortly after the conference was *The Greatest Salesman in the World* by Og Mandino. The title initially put me off, but once I read it through, the book changed my life. Mandino's book has now sold over fifty million copies, translated into twenty-five languages, and is still in print after forty-plus years. I am not going to give away the secret of the book, but I can say there is an enticing invitation to live the principles in the book through the application of some ancient scrolls that contained the secrets of success.

One scroll is titled, "I will greet this day with love in my heart." Mandino wrote, "For this is the greatest secret of success in all ventures. Muscle can split a shield and even destroy life but only the unseen power of love can open the hearts of men and until I master this art I will remain no more than a peddler in the market place. I will make love my greatest weapon and none on whom I call can defend against its force."

Another scroll is titled, "I will persist until I succeed." Mandino explained, "I was not delivered unto this world in defeat, nor does failure course in my veins. I am not a sheep waiting to be prodded by my shepherd. I am a lion and I refuse to talk, to walk, to sleep with the sheep. I will hear not those who weep and complain, for their disease is contagious. Let them join the sheep. The slaughterhouse of failure is not my destiny."

I am not alone in my opinion of Og Mandino's small book. Actor Matthew McConaughey said the same thing: "It changed my life."

REACH BEYOND YOUR GRASP

Let me take a moment and thank the hundreds of conference speakers and authors who have fed my thinking, feelings, and life. They inspired me and helped me believe in me. They encouraged me to become my possibility. They called me to extend my reach just beyond my grasp. They wanted me to win and succeed and did their best to show me how. But the big takeaway is they truly wanted me to win. Me. This is love in action. This same desire is what permeates my soul as I write to you.

Like you, it took decades of hard exploration, intense seeking, and great failure before I finally found my lifelong calling to be an executive coach and speaker. After twenty-two years I am happy to report this career choice has been better than my wildest dreams. As I look back, coaching was a crazy idea. I was the only one I knew doing executive coaching at the time. When I began back in 1997 everyone asked me, "What does an executive coach do?" I had to find creative ways to explain emotional quotient coaching and experiential learning. My coaching career began on August 4, 1997, when I got the first call. For six months my partner and I had been mailing a six-page snail-mail letter to thousands of CEOs offering them a free two-hour coaching session, in their office, and I would pay the expenses to come see them. I called this a test drive of executive coaching.

Since then, I have flown to dozens of cities to do this free initial consult. The most painful one was when I flew to New York to deliver a two-hour test drive at my own expense, and the CEO didn't move forward.

After six months of mailings, still no takers. I knew that most of the snail-mail letters went into the secretaries' round files because we weren't reaching the CEO. Desperate and determined, I began to follow up each introductory letter with a direct email to the CEO. The subject line read, "I am following up on the proposal I sent you last week." The proposal was the two-hour test drive of my coaching work.

The body of the email captured the main points of the letter and highlighted the free two-hour test drive.

The first call to come in was from a CEO of a high-tech start-up with about thirty-five employees. We'll call him Steven. He started out by saying, "I don't suffer fools well, but I will take a chance that this is worthwhile."

At the end of our two hours together, he told me that he wanted to engage my services and move forward. He asked me how much it would cost, so he could tell accounting to prepare a purchase order. I took a wild stab in the dark and quoted $1,800 per session. I kept my best poker face, as he dismissively said, "Fine. Fine. Just call Helen, my admin. She schedules my calendar."

As I was about to touch the door to leave, he called out, "Oh, one more thing." (I thought, here we go, I knew it was too good to be true.) "Lose the suit and tie, this is high tech."

That was the last time I would wear a tie for two decades. On the drive home, I pounded the steering wheel and screamed with joy. I was earning $900 an hour. At that moment I just knew I could get more CEOs to hire me.

That first client was a blessing by God. I didn't realize it, but Steven was a highly respected young rock star in the high-tech world. After a couple of months of coaching, I asked Steven if he would be willing to give me a one-paragraph testimonial about the value he was receiving from our work together. He happily agreed.

When I mailed the next batch of introductory letters, I included Steven's testimonial paragraph with his full name and company. Within a month I landed three new clients. They all said, "If you are coaching Steven, you must really be good."

Finally, the glove fit. I was forty-four years old and had found my career. I loved it then, and I love it to this day. Coaching and me—we are like peanut butter and jelly. I don't work; I get to play in making a difference in people's lives in a deep way. Don't tell any of my clients, but if I could, I would coach them for free—well almost all of them anyway. But I have found that if the client doesn't pay much, they don't listen much either. The more they pay, the more they hang on my every word, and the more they follow my advice. Thus, I have always made it a point to be the highest paid coach in the business.

After intensely working with 4,500 executives over two decades I found most of them were lost—even the CEOs didn't feel they had found their perfect fit. Often, they were in their role because it was the next right and logical career step. Maybe they were good at what they did and were offered the role of CEO. Being a CEO for many executives was not an emotional goal; in fact, it was more of a logical decision. But sometimes, despite the success and the promotions, they lacked real passion for their job, their people, or even their product offering.

They sometimes told me, "I chose this company because the technology looked interesting and showed signs of potential in the marketplace. So I am here." That's startlingly far from, "I am passionate about what I do. I love this product and this space. I love the people I work with. I can't wait to get to work every morning."

Because there was little passion in their hearts, some CEOs often did less than spectacularly well in their jobs. But for them it made no sense to leave a high-paying job as CEO for another one that was unknown. One of my first tasks was to help them find their passion.

I started by asking these questions:

- What is your personal vision for your own future?
- What do you want to accomplish?
- Describe what you want as if it were already present in your life.
    - ~ Money
    - ~ Fame
    - ~ Glory
    - ~ Prestige
    - ~ Recognition

- What would you need to achieve to make it feel as if you've reached something worthwhile to you?
- Basically, what do you passionately want?

Out of 4,500 clients, only a handful ever had a real answer. Often, their attempts to answer sounded something like, "Oh gosh, I don't know. I guess it's what most people want. I want to lead this company to a successful outcome."

A mild wish but not really a vision. And certainly not a goal at all. "Successful outcome" is ambiguous, uninspiring, and an impossible concept to form into any specific strategy. Yet, I am grateful for their answers, because it's where we start.

HOW ABOUT YOU?

- How are you feeling about your career and family?
- Does your life give you goose bumps?
- Do you feel as if your life is operating on autopilot, and as a result, do you honestly feel a little lost?
- Or do you wake up in the morning and feel as if you can't wait to get to work?
- Do you have a goal in mind that drives you to a plan, that leads you and your company in the direction you deeply desire to go?
- Are you courageous enough to even look, and then be honest with yourself about these questions? Or, what is more common, you read these lines and just keep reading?
- Or are you in a trance, going about your day uninspired, going through the motions of duty and tactics, just hoping that things will turn out okay?

If you feel okay, but only okay, it could be the job, but it's more than likely you. Your past emotional baggage may be preventing you from dreaming and believing in yourself and a brilliant future. It's a little early in this book to decide which. Just come clean with yourself about how you authentically feel about where you are, who you are, and what you want. Then keep reading. We will sort this out as we move through the pages to come.

Just know this today: You can have a life full of success, glory, satisfaction, and fulfillment regardless of your age. Heck, Colonel Sanders started his KFC restaurant chain using the money from his social security check. So don't lose heart with the wasted past. Take a deep look at where you are, then contrast it with where you would like to be in your life.

TAKEAWAYS

- It is critical for you to connect with people, movies, anything from anyone to find your passion.
- The statistical odds are against you. If only 3 percent of people achieve massive success, then you have to think, believe, and act differently.
- The main key to success in your family, love, and material life will be found in connection with others, not just speaking to them from your point of view.
- We must find our own way to learn to love others. I will show you how I did this a little later.
- It is important to make a decision to change your life. It all starts with a decision. Change can only occur after you have

decided. When that decision is made, then passion can turn your decision to change into resolve.

- Success is not easy. Once a decision is made, passion is found, and resolve is present, then you will take bold steps toward your future. Nothing changes in your external world without action.
- Dream big. Steve Jobs, the CEO of Apple, put it best: "Stay hungry, stay foolish."
- At some point in your diligent and consistent action, you will turn the corner and catch a break and the world will open up to you. You will find your Steven.
- It is critical for you to discover what you really want in life. To be able to share a story of your personal vision.
- There will be ups and downs in your journey. Roll with the punches because you will reap the rewards in the good times, and you will learn valuable lessons in the bad times.

4

THE GLORY OF IGNORANCE

I had no idea how hard life and my career would be, or how long it would take to find my nirvana career and reach substantial success, but at age nineteen, when I attended my first motivational seminar, I didn't care. My passion for creating success at something was so much larger than my fear. I embraced that I got to take it on and boldly took responsibility in finding my dream career.

I listened to early advice to try everything, which resulted in a career path that did not proceed in a straight line. My career trajectory was erratic and often aimless. Most of the time, I knew some of my jobs weren't the perfect fit, but at least I was following my heart. As Steve Jobs put it, I was staying foolish. Sometimes I needed to take a job to provide for my family, but I knew I would learn something new, and I always did.

Sometimes I learned about personalities. I saw past emotional wounds in others and how that pain spurred conflict. Every now and then I was surprised by kindness and witnessed the struggle of validation, the tension of always needing to be right. I observed how people reacted to failure and how they responded to success. I learned about customers and the dynamics of why they bought.

Every job brought in new information and added to my experiences. And I began to see that success was about passionate resolve acted out through relationships.

I LEARNED TO BE CREATIVE

I eventually earned the position of VP of sales and marketing for a building security equipment manufacturer. I had spent considerable time trying to land a big prospect, Ademco. They were based in Syosset, New York. Ademco was a huge distributor with hundreds of retail outlets across the country. They were the big gun in this space.

Frank Owen was Ademco's main buyer. I had been calling on him for almost a year. We always came to an impasse on price. He wanted a price of $1.00 for a special little part called a magnetic contact. It was a simple hermetically sealed magnetic rhodium-plated reed switch. It was a commodity product that told the burglar alarm control panel if a door was open or closed.

During my entire tenure at the company, the CEO adhered to the main goal, which would not be compromised, of a net profit of 24 percent on all sold parts. The parts sold for $1.28 each. To meet my boss's goal of 24 percent net, in the face of my customer's need for a sale price of $1.00 a part, the impasse seemed impossible to break. The numbers just didn't work.

But I was committed to landing this big fish. I did a lot of pondering on this dilemma and told my boss that I would go to Syosset and close the sale. He told me it would never happen, and if I brought back a PO that didn't reveal a path to 24 percent net profit, he would reject the order. I proposed a bet. If I closed the sale, and the PO was approved, he would pay for a week-long trip to Cancun, first class all the way. My boss just smiled and agreed because he thought I couldn't win.

When I arrived in Frank's office at Ademco, I told him that I would meet his price of $1.00, but he had to accommodate some special requirements. I explained that the initial order had to be for one million parts over a short period of time. I told him that I didn't want to just stuff the channel so I needed to train his employees on our products with a training day. These trainings in each retail location would be done on my time schedule, so his people would know how and why to sell our products. This arrangement enabled me to create a circular path on long trips, rather than make random back-and-forth flights.

I told him that I wanted four full-color ads in his monthly catalog at no cost to me to help move the product off the shelf. I also told him that I wanted end-cap display space in each of his retail outlets. And finally, I told him that he would have to agree to pay our invoices at "net 10 days" for every invoice.

Frank agreed. I waited in the lobby for the purchase order and then flew home.

When I got to my office, I raced in to the CEO and told him that I closed the sale.

He said, "No way."

I handed over the PO. He took one look at the $1.00 price and tossed it on the table. "I am not accepting this. I told you we needed 24 percent net profit. We talked about this."

I said, "Just hear me out."

I explained that our fixed costs for manufacturing will remain the same with or without the order. But if we take the order, the economies of scale kick in. I checked with purchasing; our raw material costs could be lowered with this volume by 25 percent for all our manufacturing for this part, to all our other customers. If we started a second shift in the factory, only our variable costs would increase, and both of these principles empower more profitability.

In fact, our total costs would be lowered to the point that by taking the order at $1.00 we would actually make more profit from our overall sales. This is because our lowered material costs and added variable labor cost would be realized across all our manufacturing. After about twenty minutes, he shook my hand and told me to enjoy my trip to Cancun.

It's a powerful example of how ignorance of what can and can't be done opens up our creative possibility. The trip to Cancun was exhilarating, starting with the limo ride to the airport.

The moral of that story is that I didn't know how I was going to be able to succeed until near the end. It was my blind, dogged commitment driven by passion that made me take step after step to discover how I actually could succeed.

Commitment fueled by passion opens the door to creative epiphanies. It is through these epiphanies we find the path to massive success. Now when I hear "it can't be done," I smile. Og Mandino's book, *The Greatest Salesman in the World*, stated, "Failure cannot overtake you, if your desire to succeed is strong enough.

WHAT DO YOU WANT TO DO WHEN YOU GROW UP?

A blessed few among us have always known what they wanted to do with their lives. If you happen to be one of those few who as a child always wanted to be a fireman, and then ultimately became one and felt at home, fantastic for you. But for most of us humans, this is not the case.

I have asked thousands of college-age men and women what they want as a career. Almost without exception, they tell me they don't know, or at least they are not sure. This is natural, common, and perfect. But if there is a deliberateness about their search, I know they will be just fine. The important point is that they are on their journey and seeking their truth—a truth that actually constantly evolves.

I have a friend we will call Julio. After high school, Julio went to college to be a pharmacist. After graduation he began his career. It didn't take long for him to realize that pharmacy wasn't for him. He told me, "There came a moment pretty much right away that I realized most of my day was reduced to counting pills."

Julio is a Type A personality, driven, personable, and passionate at his core. Pharmacy was never going to work for him. Julio entered the world of real estate. But in a big way, by raising money from limited partners and buying apartment and condo complexes. Julio would raise enough money to go in, remodel, and then raise rents. The strategy was to hold the newly improved property for a few years, continue to improve the property and raise rents, and then sell at a profit. Take the original money, plus profit, and buy more and bigger properties. Julio has been at this now for a few decades, and I am not sure, but he's probably worth $100+ million. Instead of counting pills, he counts properties.

My wife, Kathleen, and I were in a little country store during a trip we took a couple of years ago. The store had cute little sayings on homemade signs on the wall. One caught my eye and made me chuckle: "Now that you're 18, leave home while you still know everything." That was how I felt at eighteen. I knew what I knew, and I knew I was right. Of course, most often I was not. But that was okay because I still felt I was right, and this feeling kept me moving forward.

I was wrong, of course—a lot. What mattered was that I was boldly moving forward. It was this certainty about what I thought I knew that kept me going. If I had understood all of what I didn't know, I might have just sat back and waited to learn what to do next.

Of course there was some wreckage or broken glass in the rear-view mirror of my life, which, at the time, was sharp and cutting. But even that was perfect. We live in an imperfect world and are imperfect human beings.

Looking back, I had deep regrets about some of my decisions because they wound up hurting others. But I got to clean them up over time. While I would never want to go through the pain of my bad decisions again, I wouldn't change any part of my journey because it equipped me to be here with who I am and where I am today.

There is brilliance in ignorance. The brilliance is that you believe in yourself, which is the fuel to drive forward, make mistakes, get humble, and then learn. Often in youth you haven't been deeply hurt much, so you are not afraid of consequences. You combine your passion with certainty that you know what you want, and how to get it, and these beliefs help make you unstoppable.

Can you look back in your life and see that your ignorance enabled you to attempt things that ultimately benefited your career today? That you gained something valuable from even the most painful decisions?

Life's challenges, including your youthful mistakes, will either catapult you into success or drive the adventure right out of you. When bad things happen, you either see them as lessons to be learned, or you stop in your tracks and blame others for your hurt. You become a victim. The stories we write in our head about the pain in life determine the direction of our emotions.

The elusive holy grail is, of course, to have the experience and wisdom that comes from making a lot of good and bad decisions, coupled with the blind, bold passion of youth. To a great extent, you can have both, but when life deals you a blow, you have to rediscover your inner passion to dream again in order to ignite new possibilities.

A truism in flying is this: A pilot tries to be aware of the closest landing strip all the time. In the event of a mechanical problem, in addition to working the problem, at some point the pilot searches for some kind of runway. It may be a field or a golf course, but a landing spot will almost always appear. Many times, when a plane is in trouble, the pilot will only focus on the gauges and working the switches until there is no time to find a runway. Then they crash. It's important to work the problem, but you also need to be aware of the solution. In this case the solution could be a field.

When you believe that a solution to a problem exists—and believe you will find it in time to land the plane—almost always you will discover a place to land, and almost always just in time to save the day.

Does a solution always happen? No. But does believing that a solution exists somewhere ahead of time help leverage a positive outcome? Yes. When it doesn't happen that you find your solution in time, is that also perfect? Yes. Sometimes it's critical to suffer through the "crash" to find humility, to finally see the need to dramatically change your direction and create a fresh start.

This can make you crazy if you are not careful. But here is the point. We can embrace that whatever happens, happens. Everything in your life is just an event. It's the meaning that we create about the event where there is negative or positive power found in our lives.

A popular story of a boy and a Zen master is told in the movie *Charlie Wilson's War*. Here's how the story is told:

Did I ever tell you the story of the Zen master and the little boy? On his sixteenth birthday, a boy gets a horse as a present. All the villagers say, "How wonderful!"

The Zen master says, "We'll see."

One day, the boy is thrown from the horse and is hurt and can no longer walk. All the villagers say, "How terrible!"

The Zen master says, "We'll see."

A short time later, war begins, and all the young men of the village are taken away to be soldiers, but this boy can't fight, so he is spared, and all the villagers say, "How wonderful!"

And the Zen master says, "We'll see."

The point is this: When something bad happens, it's only bad because we attach that meaning to it. The event itself can be neither good nor bad. It only becomes so because we say so. When we disassociate meaning from events, we will find that there is no pain there. We actually learn from everything we experience in our lives. So embrace the glory and the pain. Because you grow from both.

As I mature, I strive to combine the wisdom of experience with the boldness of passion, which empowers me to still power forward in the face of risk, especially when I can't see the outcome.

A dear friend of mine was a dentist in Mt. Shasta, California. Dr. Don Ratley. We were both in Rotary and took on building a free dental clinic in Mulege, Mexico. This dental center was actually a remodel of an existing building. The center was going to provide free dental care for the people of the village and surrounding area.

After it was built, Rotarian dentists from around the country would fly in for a week with their families. The dentist would provide free dental care from 8:00 a.m. to noon, then have the afternoons off to spend with their families. The next week a different dentist and their family would fly in and take over the work and the fun. Fifty-two dentists served one week each, which provided free dental care for the population.

Bob Keeline, Clair Carter, and I were the advance team to go in and get the site ready for the build. It was the late 1970s, and Bob owned a plane. It was a single-engine Cessna 182 Skylane with fixed landing gear. Mulege is about halfway down the Baja Peninsula on the Sea of Cortez side.

When I got to the plane before takeoff in California, I noticed that the fiberglass skirts over the wheels had been removed. Then I noticed that the backseat was removed to fill the plane with construction tools. A pad tossed over the pile of tools was my "business class" recliner.

As we flew out of Calexico, California, Bob threw a paper map of Baja over his shoulder and said, "Look at the map and then look out of the window for landmarks you identify on the map. Pay attention to the paved road below as it bends left and right. Notice the landmarks, landscape, and shoreline. Track where we are all the way down to Mulege."

As he was instructing me, he was tapping on an instrument that was showing a red flag inside one of the gauges.

"What's that for?" I asked.

He told me that it was a directional indicator that takes us from one airport to another. Since they don't have this technology down here, the gauge was letting him know that, without a signal, it has turned off. I, with a paper map, instantly became the sole navigator. He told me to especially take note of the little airstrips on the map that were sprinkled across the terrain and track our location relevant to them. If we had any trouble, I was to tell him if the nearest airstrip was behind us or ahead of us.

There should have been drinks in this business class.

As we were on final approach, he told me he was glad that he removed the fiberglass skirts from the wheels because the dirt runway was rough. We were descending to within ten feet of the dirt runway, and I noticed that we were moving left and then right randomly. I asked if he was fighting a crosswind.

He said, "No. I am avoiding the ruts." I am still grateful that we missed hitting the dog that ran across the runway in front of us moments after we touched down.

After we landed, we taxied to fill up with gas. I discovered that he had done his homework (wisdom). He pulled a pair of pantyhose out of his flight bag and covered the nozzle of the fuel spout. After filling he pulled the nozzle out of the wing tank. It was then I noticed a small mound of grit hanging inside the pantyhose. That grit would have gone into our wing tanks. Thanks, Bob, for your foresight to bring pantyhose for our flight.

Then he proceeded to put a glass vial into an orifice on the bottom of the wing. This was intended to bleed off any water droplets that may have been in the airport's fuel tanks. It was large enough to maybe collect 4 ounces of unwanted water. When he was done, he had emptied the 4-ounce container three times. Bob's wisdom again.

Bob was elegantly coping with the limitations that stood in the way of our getting what we wanted, and that was safe fuel. He didn't require the perfect fuel, or the smoothest runway. Instead he was prepared to create a safe landing and extract perfect fuel. Bob was bold enough to fly to Mulege, but wise enough to make sure we got home safely. This is passion and boldness coupled with wisdom.

Sure there was subtle fear of the unknown that Bob Keeline must have experienced before we took off. But it was his passion and commitment to successfully fly us to a dirt airstrip in Mexico and back home safely that made him consider what needed to be done in preparation, and his courage to face the unknowns with creativity, that carried the day.

IGNORANCE AND SERENDIPITY

So be bold. Follow your heart. Before Steve Jobs, the founder and CEO of Apple, dropped out of college, before he started Apple with Steve Wozniak, he was still interested in learning. One day he passed by a calligraphy class. Intrigued, he audited the class. He learned about fonts, kerning, leading, and style. He had no idea how this would help his career; he just followed his heart.

Later, what he learned was fantastically important to making the Mac a success. It was Steve Jobs's passion and drive coupled with what he fell in love with in the calligraphy class that made the Apple computer have color and different fonts in different sizes. Do you think that these had anything to do with beating the PC for the home computer market?

Then there was the time Steve was visiting Xerox Park, the research and development arm of Xerox. A developer was working on something that caught Steve's eye. When asked, the developer told him that it was a new way to navigate a computer. They called it "drag and drop" instead of command-line coding instruction.

Steve asked what Xerox was planning to do with it. The answer was a shrugged shoulder. Steve asked if he could have the software. The answer was "Why not?" How foolish was it for Steve to spend time at Xerox Park? How crazy and bold was it for Steve to ask them to give him the drag and drop software for free? Oh, the glory of blind ignorance coupled with bold passion!

During the dot-com era, I was coaching a new CEO of an infant start-up. We'll call him Bill. Twenty-two-year-old Bill was a good guy at heart and was focused on doing the right thing. He graduated from Stanford and within three months had secured venture funding from Sand Hill Road for himself and his two other founders' new idea. Sand Hill Road is where most of the big venture capitalists in Silicon Valley call home.

Back in the dot-com days, money was free. No one had problems securing venture funding for almost any kind of high-tech start-up, and Bill was no exception.

But this was Bill's first job of any kind, and suddenly he was the CEO. He and two of his friends had a brilliant idea and raised money to start the company, but managing it was a whole different deal. The company was about three months old when Bill asked me to coach him. Bill's first questions caught me off guard. Then I remembered that this was his first job ever.

He asked me, "How often should my executive team meet?" I answered once a week. "When should I hold these meetings?" I suggested Monday mornings at 9:00 a.m. "What should we talk about during these meetings?"

I gave him the fundamentals to these questions:

- When will projects be completed?
- Who is taking the lead on each item to accomplish?
- What is the status of development on each project?
- What are the obstacles we are facing?
- How much money will be required to complete each project?
- Who will be our target market?
- What will be our ASP (average sales price)?
- Why will they buy our solution?
- What do we think our "bill of materials" cost will be?
- How much margin should we expect at an average sales price of what?
- Is there any competition for our solution, and how will we successfully win a majority of the prospects?

The company had now grown to about twelve people with three VPs and Bill as the CEO. About six months into our engagement, he reluctantly shared: "My VP of marketing and I were in New York last week for some meetings. She is twenty-two years old, like me. I guess we both knew we were attracted to each other, and we even joked about it. The first night we were in the elevator on the way up to our separate rooms, and one thing led to another and we started kissing. It was all consensual. Well you can imagine the rest of the story. We spent the night together."

I asked if he was interested in her as a romantic relationship?

He said yes. But he was also worried it was a mistake. I told him that his assessment of the event was right. He continued to explain he had been avoiding her the last couple of days because he knew his actions were not in the best interest of the company. "Now she is getting upset that I am not showing signs of pursuing our romantic relationship. In fact, I think she has told someone in the company about our dalliance."

I said, "No judgment here, but you have destroyed your ability to lead this direct report as her boss. It's now nearly impossible for you to reprimand her for anything she does poorly. And this relationship will and probably has gone viral in the company. As a result, it will be difficult to give her a raise, promotion, or a bonus without people judging you as taking care of your girlfriend."

I cautioned him, "Because you are the CEO, this can erupt quickly into a political then legal problem putting the entire company's future at risk. It doesn't take much for a twenty-two-year-old who already is feeling shunned by you to get angry and file a sexual harassment lawsuit. It is easier for a venture capital firm to shut down a six-month-old company that hasn't yet finished one product but is embroiled in a sexual harassment lawsuit than to stand by you."

I asked him about his signing authority. "Up to $50,000 without board approval."

I recommended he draft the $50,000 check that day, prepare the legal waiver and agreement to never sue for sexual harassment or anything else in the future, then meet with her at the end of the day.

"Show her the check, ask her to sign the waiver, and separate her from employment," I advised. "Tell her ruining your ability to maintain a boss/direct report relationship was all your fault. Since it's the dot-com era, you can help her find a job by tomorrow morning. And if you meant what you said about your interest in her as a romantic relationship, tell her that you would like to start dating."

He did what I suggested, and she agreed. There was never a problem. The company grew and enjoyed a liquidity event. She found a good job in three days, plus was $50,000 richer. She and Bill even dated for a short time. Because of the way the situation was handled, the winner was the young lady. As it should have been.

It was Bill, the CEO, who was wrong, and he intuitively knew it. Bill didn't know a lot about leading or even running a company. But he quickly learned. His ambition, passion, and commitment brought him to a place of courage to discover, act, and do the right thing in the face of ignorance.

Many bright twenty-two-year-old grads got funded to start companies and didn't know anything about business. But through boldness coupled with ignorance, they raised money and started new enterprises. In most cases, their experiences in the dot-com era failed, but most went on to take cool VP roles in other companies and did well. Their wild experience in the crazy dot-com world ended up as a crash course in business leadership. Out of those early crashes, no one starved to death or became homeless. But they all learned a great deal.

From 1997 to 2000, venture capitalists told me they would never hire a CEO over thirty-five years old. "They just don't get the new internet economy." But many of these young CEOs were business maturity infants. I frequently felt like I was a kindergarten executive coach.

After the dot-com crash, and after the valley lost over a trillion dollars, those same venture capitalists declared, "I am not funding any company with a CEO under the age of thirty-five. They need to have some maturity and experience to build a solid business." I just nodded and smiled.

USE YOUR HEAD—AND YOUR HEART

The problem with experience is that it's wasted on old men and women. By the time you get wisdom, you also know all the reasons why something won't work, and often in the later years, the energy to do it anyway is waning.

It drives me crazy how we excessively honor the perception of using just the intellect. Researchers even discovered that, in a meeting, attendees consistently identify the critic as the smartest person in the room, the person who always voices several reasons why something can't be done. And to look smart, the critic doesn't even need to offer a plan on how to succeed; they only need to criticize.

Young adults don't have a lot of experiences to draw on. In our youth, most of our decisions are made with our emotions. If I asked you the question, "Who is generally more passionate, the young or the old?" you would say the young. I believe that when we are young, we use our heart to decide our course of action. As we mature, we tend to use our brain because we are trained to use our brain. How many times has a parent or teacher asked you, "How do you feel about this?" You would probably say never.

Yet for truly sustainable success, we need to use both the brain and the heart equally.

If a formally trained mind is so critical to success, how is it that college dropouts Bill Gates, Larry Ellison, Michael Dell, and Steve Jobs succeeded? Now please don't read me wrong here. A formal education is fantastically powerful. But when we rely solely on what we have learned, and not on what we intuitively feel, we greatly limit our chances for success.

As a society we are driven to teach our youth to use their brain, not their heart. What were we told growing up?

- Grow up.
- Use your head.
- Do the right thing.
- Think it through.
- Act your age.
- Don't be foolish.

Traditional schools educate the brain but totally discount the need for the awareness or input of the emotions. Did you ever take a class that taught you how to leverage your emotions in order to ignite passion, which would result in commitment and bold actions? Of course not. I have heard hundreds of clients ask, “Why don’t they teach this in college?” The reason is that in the US, we are uncomfortable talking about emotions. We have incredibly strong intellectual muscles, but our emotional muscles are atrophied due to a lack of understanding and neglect.

We have three parts to our being. We have body, mind, and spirit (emotions). Why are these three classified in this order? It is because they have been prioritized by our society from most to least important. We go to the gym for the body. We get degrees in higher learning at institutions to feed and train our intellect. But how have we been trained to feed our emotional life? We have not. So we operate using less than all the tools in our toolbox. And I will say that the emotional muscle is the most important by far in creating any kind of success.

About ten years ago I had a client, Jackson, who had developed some amazing technology. The focus of the marketing strategy was in the automotive space. The company had struggled for four years to enter the automotive market, yet had been unsuccessful. It was always, “We have several design wins, and everyone loves our technology, but no one has placed an order.”

The company had raised three rounds of venture funding and had almost burned through all of it. Jackson shared that he was scared about raising another round of financing based on a story that had generated no market traction.

I asked Jackson if his heart was in this technology for this market. He answered no.

Well, that was telling, so I followed up and asked why Jackson hadn’t shifted the technology that he was indeed excited about to a new market. He told me that if he even suggested starting over, the board would run for the exit. No one would want to acknowledge that everything from the beginning until now was somewhat of a waste. I got it. But I told him that without his enrollment in the promise that the market holds for his company, it would be nearly impossible to succeed.

I asked him to picture what he would do with the technology if he could do anything. He told me about his deep passion for the gaming space. I spent some time helping him to experience this passion as if it were already successful there. His passion grew to the point of commitment. He finally followed his heart and developed a pitch deck for the board featuring the company's technology in gaming.

He was humble, but honest about what he perceived about the company's future in the automotive industry for their product. Yes, there was gnashing of teeth, and a couple board members did head for the exit. But the rest of the board enrolled with the new vision. They did a new round with a new lead investor and launched. It was a great success. After a couple of years, Jackson sold the company for a handsome sum and moved on with passion and courage to his next new thing.

Thoughts create emotions. Once our thoughts are supported by aligned emotions, both drive our attitudes, actions, behaviors, and words. Looked at another way, our thoughts ultimately lead to outcomes, so in the final analysis, our thoughts eventually and inevitably become our reality. More on this idea in a few moments.

Most people feel lost, and because of this feeling and the stories they have created in their mind, they feel stuck. And they can't admit it, because it would bring up an emotion they don't want to feel—namely, that they don't know what to do. They feel the position of CEO means they should always know what to do next. They certainly don't want to feel stupid because they can't figure it out. We are embarrassed by feeling and especially by showing emotion. Being emotional looks like immaturity; it looks weak. Yet emotion is the most critical part of our lives.

Thoughts. The summation or collection of our thoughts dictates the emotions we feel. If I were to watch a half hour of Fox News, then turn the channel and watch a half hour of MSNBC, I would turn off the TV and feel, "As a country, we are screwed." On the other hand, if I were to listen to a podcast by business optimist Simon Sinek or Lisa Nichols for an hour, I would feel inspired. The collection of our sequential thoughts always leads to an emotion, either positive or negative.

Feelings. Feelings always lead to actions, words, and behaviors. "I didn't feel like doing it" or "I know I should have done this or that but didn't want to." How many times have you known what to do, chosen to do it, even committed to do it, like a diet, only to fail? The knowledge or reasoning to do a task isn't enough. We have to want to do a thing. Like it or not, most of us do what we want.

Actions, words, and behaviors over time always render our result. If you want to change your outcome in life, you have to act, speak, and behave differently than you are today. You can't do the same thing the same way and expect a different result.

What do you control in your life? Really. If I were with you in person, we would examine the principle that we control nothing except one thing: our thoughts. You don't directly control your emotions. It's difficult to be joyous on demand. We don't control our actions, words, and behaviors either.

Do you control your actions? Well, have you ever had to apologize for something you did? You may have felt at the time that maybe you shouldn't do it, but you did anyway? Have you ever had to apologize for something you said? Have you ever been a jerk to someone because you were having a bad day? Just like me, of course, you have.

The only action we control is our thoughts. You have the power to control your thoughts in this moment. Let me prove it. Right now, I want you to think about your left foot. Wiggle your toes and feel your foot. You see, I can even control your thoughts in the moment. You can, too, all day, all the time. It's called mindfulness for a reason. It takes tons of practice, and it's hard work. But it will change your life wildly. Is this constant work to control your thoughts worth changing your life to what you want? Only you can answer that, but what else do you have planned for the rest of your life? May as well plan to get what you want.

By controlling your thoughts and choosing to focus on solutions instead of being stuck in the problem, you will empower better ideas, create positive self-talk, repeat inspirational stories, follow passionate goals, and find and nurture love. When you do this over a short period of time, like a couple of hours, you will feel positive and inspired. When you make this a disciplined habit, it will become more natural. When it becomes more natural, the practice begins to modify your personality. When you feel powerful and inspired, you automatically take powerful and inspired actions, and speak powerfully and inspiringly. When you act, speak, and behave powerfully over time, you get powerful and inspiring results.

By the way, even without the material rewards, living this way is completely worth it, even without the results. If you practice controlling your thoughts over time, it becomes a more natural way to be, and this alters your perceptions of life and who you truly are. You can change your personality over time.

If you want to change your life, begin by changing your thoughts. It's the only tool you have to leverage your emotions and beliefs, which will automatically drive your actions. And if you are still stuck, there is another power you may consider. Sometimes things just seem like an anchor too heavy to lift out of the sand.

Maybe the God of your understanding could help. I don't mean religion or church. By the way, I hate religion, I love God. What I am referring to is the God of your understanding, should you happen to believe. Talk to your God. Ask for direction. If you are riled up now because I mentioned God, sorry. What you believe or not believe is completely okay with me. I have found in my personal experience, for me, that there is great power in deploying both my mind and my spiritual side when I am seeking difficult and deep answers.

Every now and then things happen in our lives that can be too much for us to handle. Like the loss of a child or a divorce. In these times I need a power greater than myself.

IGNORANCE ISN'T BLISS, BUT IT CAN BE BENEFICIAL

In summary, your ignorance can be a huge benefit. Ignorance lets you try foolish follies and fail. Then you become humble. When you are humble, you learn. I can't learn a thing if I am certain I'm already right. I only become open in my mind when I finally admit I don't have the answer. Ignorance makes you open to new ideas and solutions if you are humble. In fact, you are nothing but a creative possibility when you are ignorant.

Find your passion to move forward in order to learn. When you maintain your passion over the decades with this learning, you will become massively successful. That is my goal for you—to become massively successful in your business life as well as personal life, so you can enjoy your success.

But remember, success is an inside job. It is almost never about external circumstances. When you feel the inner you is successful, then all the fruits of success will show up on the outside. You will attract all the success you dare to dream of.

TAKEAWAYS

- As you go through life, you will experience successes and failures. Don't miss the opportunity to learn with the setbacks. They are incredibly valuable going forward.
- Don't let the rules stop you. Stay inside honesty and integrity and still dig for a creative answer. I guarantee you there is almost always one there. Be creative, stay with the goal.

- Like Julio, when you find yourself in a career space where you have no passion, leave. Do something else. Don't let momentum keep you stuck.
- Ignorance is a gift if it helps you get out of the logical brain and get on an adventure.
- Sell yourself that there is always a runway when you need a place to land.
- Preparation for the obstacles that might occur can make your journey a lot safer.
- When you discover that you made a mistake, like something that started in an elevator, take responsibility, and take care of those you've harmed. In this way, nothing comes back to bite you.
- Find the courage to follow your heart, and do what you feel is best, especially when it's scary. Jackson teaches us that when we follow our heart, we just might win. When we don't, failure is almost certain, and then you do have something to blame yourself for.
- The thoughts that you allow yourself to think are the only steering wheel you have.
- Thoughts drive feelings, and feelings drive actions, words, and behaviors. These drive your outcome.
- If you find yourself ignorant of what to do next, that's great. Ignorance brings humility. We only learn when we are humble.

5

TRANSFORM PAIN INTO A CATALYST FOR SUCCESS

Pain is a natural occurrence in life. It can't be avoided. And it shouldn't be. Lots of events in life are painful, but it doesn't mean they are not worth experiencing. In fact, it's often the painful experiences that benefit us the most. Because through pain we often learn and grow.

Can we agree that childbirth must be painful to a mom? But birth is still a beautiful thing. Is watching your daughter get married to a wonderful man painful for a father? Of course. These are just two instances where pain is natural, worth it, and actually good and beautiful.

But our ego's job is to protect us from pain, pretty much at all cost. When you face taking a calculated risk to seek success, usually the ego is screaming in your head, no! It is telling you about all the things that could go wrong, and how you might suffer embarrassment or defeat.

Learning to embrace pain as a natural human experience will serve you well in your quest for a successful life. In fact, since emotional pain is a part of creating any kind of success, it is best embraced, and embraced to be faced over a sustained period of time.

One of the greatest lessons I have learned working with over 400 companies is that our success in everything is dependent on our ability to embrace and endure pain, and then transform that pain into a catalyst for success. What do I mean?

Let's start with an example: sales. You make ten sales calls and get nine *nos* for each *yes*. A natural part of sales is that it's a numbers game.

Can you endure nine *nos* and still maintain your passion to find the one *yes*? Prospecting for a sale involves more than just enduring *no*. It often includes feedback like "I am not interested in the product."

This *no* that we hear is often interpreted incorrectly as you, the salesperson, is not interesting enough for me to listen to what you have to offer. I am not interested in you. You are not worth my time to get to know you through listening to you. In fact, you are an unwanted distraction to my busy day. I am happy with the company I currently deal with and happy with their product. You and your offering are not as good as what I currently use. You are not wanted here. All of these statements do not represent the truth, but they are often the story written in the mind of the salesperson. It is this story that causes our pain.

We can accidentally gather a great deal of meaning behind that simple *no*.

I recently met Todd Komarnicki who wrote the screenplay for *Sully*, the movie about Chesley "Sully" Sullenberger and the miraculous landing of US Airways flight 1549 on the Hudson River. I asked Todd how many times he rewrote the screenplay to get the beautiful script it is. He replied about thirty times. He went on to tell me how much more fun it was to be a published author than to write. Can you imagine the pain involved in rewriting your entire screenplay thirty times?

How about your own personal experience with a spouse or your children? How many times do they say something that hurts? How many times have you been disappointed by them? Yet you know to achieve success as a spouse or a parent, you've got to still love them. Enduring the pain of being a spouse or a parent is part of the job description of being a spouse or a parent.

How many times have you had trouble reconciling a financial account, or finding and fixing a software bug, or getting an employee out of a funk, only to find that it takes a long time to fix these issues? How many times has something just not gone your way? How disappointed do you get looking back at the wasted time?

Do you golf? Enough said. It takes effort, practice, and lots of lost balls to improve your game. Fishing? How many times do you have to cast? How about the times your $9 lure gets tangled in reeds only to lose it before you get a bite?

As a farmer, how many times has a drought, or a flood, or an oversupplied market, or a big repair bill on a tractor dashed your dreams of financial success? As a tech start-up, how many dog and pony shows must you deliver before you find a willing lead investor?

Life is rigorous and demands you learn to embrace pain along the path. Painful experiences will continue even after you come to terms with that fact. As you know by looking around, many people do not learn. When they experience the pain that naturally comes along with striving for success, they blame others. They insist they are a victim of circumstances, or the market, or someone who did them wrong. They get bitter. They lose all power to create relationships to help them out of the quagmire. They quit. This is why most people and most companies never succeed. They capitulate to the pain. They carry their pain as a burden instead of just embracing the pain as the natural path to learning in the normal course of life.

It's only when we learn how to transform our interpretation of pain into lessons that we actually learn to grow. We learn in two ways: We learn by winning, which causes us to look back and say, "That worked, let's do more of that." And we learn by failing. We get to say, "That didn't work. What can I learn from that experience that will equip me for success at the next attempt?" We learn from both winning and losing. If you want success, seek both.

When we see life as it truly is, we then, and only then, are able to embrace pain as a natural part of life. When pain does come, we frame it as an opportunity for learning. Pain is a wonderful teacher. If no pain were involved, we wouldn't pay much attention to the lesson.

You know where this is going. If you want success, embrace the fact that success comes with a lot of pain. The trick is to change the story about pain into a story about benefits and learning. Every time we learn something, we equip ourselves to enjoy greater levels of statistical success in the future, which results in fewer failures. Which means less pain. Life can actually improve as we learn to embrace pain, because when we do, pain subsides.

I have yet to encounter a client who achieved massive success without first walking through the fire of striving and losing. They did not gain on success without having to pick themselves up, over and over, marshaling a renewed vigor and passion.

How often does natural and easy success occur? Oh, I would say maybe .0001 percent of all start-ups.

I am privileged to know the intricate details of the hundreds of stories of pain, striving, slogging, and dogmatic commitment. I have watched (and helped) C-suite officers pick up, find their passion again, and drive forward to succeed. Every one of my 400 high-tech start-up CEOs and over 4,000 VP clients have endured enormous learning and challenges before their massive success. But we only hear the success stories, never the struggle.

I know and understand the ugly underbelly of stories that have consistently occurred in the background of all of my successful clients. I wish I could help you understand that where you are, and what you are going through, is perfect. What you are experiencing today is exactly what creating a massively successful company feels like.

My man Og Mandino said, "Failure can never overtake you if your desire to win is strong enough."

Now here is an example of how we can trick the ego and change the pain of no. We will call him Albert. He was the head of all retail sales for a regional newspaper. His job was to hire and train people to go out and sell ad space in his newspaper. I asked him how he did this, given that most of his salespeople had never sold anything before. He told me a story about how he circumvented the pain of no with his new salespeople.

On the first day of going and selling ad space, he told each new salesperson to take their prospect list and make twenty face-to-face sales calls every day.

He told them, "Your goal is to go out and get twenty *nos*. At the end of each day I want you to come see me and show me who you called on and why they said no. Again, the goal was to get twenty *nos*."

He said nothing about getting a sale. After a couple of days or weeks, a new salesperson would return and tell Albert that in fact they got nineteen *nos* and one sale.

He responded, "Why didn't you go out and make one more sales call so you could have achieved your goal of twenty *nos*?"

The new salespeople got it in their hearts that the goal was twenty *nos*. This took all the negativity away from getting a *no*. After a couple of months, Albert would let them off the hook of getting the twenty *nos*. By this time, each salesperson was easily walking into twenty prospects every day. Albert's goal was to get them to make the sales calls, and not let the *nos* make them slide on their requirement to make sales calls.

I loved that story then, and I love it now. We can actually restructure our perspective on a no, and turn it into a behavior modification without facing any pain of rejection. Those new salespersons' goal was to get a rejection. It was to be celebrated. Can we do the same with our daunting tasks?

TAKEAWAYS

- Pain is actually our friend. It is our teacher, not the enemy. It only becomes the enemy when we embrace the desire to avoid pain.

- Pain can have a huge reward like a new baby, or a new son-in-law, or the building of character.
- When someone tells you no, it's almost always never personal.
- Almost everything in life that holds grand value is hard. That's one big reason the end goal has grand value.
- When you are dealt a blow, don't blame. When we do, we miss the lesson the experience is holding for us. We are preoccupied with the blaming of others, so we miss the lesson.
- I once heard it said, "A person is never a failure when he or she fails; they are only a failure when they quit." So learn to embrace failure, make friends with it, because it often is your best teacher.
- Hold fast to Albert's lesson. Turn failure into something that can become a friend.

6

THE ULTIMATE WAR: FEAR VS COURAGE

Would you say that the emotion of fear is good or bad? Looked at another way, is fear profitable or a liability? The answer is yes. It can be either. For example, I love a fire in the fireplace on a cold winter night, but I hate fire outside the stove when the couch goes up in flames. So is fire good or bad? We can agree that inside the stove, fire is good; outside the stove, fire is bad.

Fear keeps our hands off the top of the stove. Fear keeps me safe on a narrow trail with a steep cliff to my right. Fear keeps me from being rude to my wife and calling her angry, hurtful names because it could cause a divorce.

Fear is a mentally fabricated emotion based on how we read our environment. Thoughts of what might occur can stir fear. The stimulus of our environment fuels the internal stories we write in our head. More concisely, the accuracy of perceived truth with which we read our environment determines whether fear is warranted or not. Fear often occurs when we misread the circumstances. This is disempowering and a liability.

Fear often makes us hesitate too long over a decision. It can cause us to play it safe when what is actually called for is boldness. When working to persuade others, fear is kryptonite. When people see we are fearful, they don't feel safe following our advice. So fear and the stories we write in our head prevent us from finding the power we need to be bold, powerful, persuasive, loving, generous, and creative.

Fear is often expressed as anger.

When I see anger present in an individual or a team, I now see it is almost always the fruit of fear. If fear is the tree, then the fruit is often anger. In my mind anger is never a root emotion. It is secondary. When I feel love for my wife, this is a root emotion. I don't need a reason to love my wife. I just love her. But if I am afraid that I will lose the love of my wife, then what often shows up is anger.

If I am angry because I was passed over for a deserved promotion, I become angry at how unjust the decision is. If I am about to lose something, like a favorite car, because I can't afford the payment, then I get angry at the boss for passing me over for a promotion. The root fear is my budget. Fear is the root emotion.

When you see anger, look for the root cause—the fear that lurks behind it all.

When we present an idea to a team, and someone shoots it down as stupid, we are afraid of looking bad to the team, and we get angry. We are angry because we fear losing the team's respect. The primary root emotion is the fear of looking bad, which triggers the secondary emotion of anger. It can also be FOMO—the Fear Of Missing Out that causes anger.

So why even address anger when the problem is fear? We all know that sometimes it is critical to address anger because the consequences of an angry person damage the team. In this instance we address anger because it can cause damage. But then we look behind the anger and search for the fear that drove it into our presence.

I don't like to engage in anger management as the end-all goal. I want to dig and find out what causes the fear in someone, which shows up as anger. People don't like to admit they are afraid, but they don't mind letting you know why they are angry. This happens all the time because anger can make you look strong, while fear is often seen as weak.

FEAR IS A SELF-FULFILLING PROPHECY

In an old study, researchers met with a group of people and recorded the answers to the question, "What worries you in the coming year?" After twelve months the researchers followed up with the participants and asked how many of their worries came true. The result was a startling 10 percent. Only 10 percent of what they worried about came to pass. Which means 90 percent of the events they worried about never happened.

My question is how many opportunities were missed that year due to their unfounded fears? How does unfounded fear cause us to play it safe? How much creativity was curtailed because of fear? And what a waste of emotional energy worrying about the 90 percent, which never came to pass.

When we write gloomy stories in our head about what is going to happen, we artificially ignite the emotion of fear. When we *think* something bad is likely to happen for too many moments in a row, we truly begin to *feel* it will happen.

When the stories in our head make our heart feel and believe the self-fabricated prophecy for doom and gloom, then we find ourselves in head and heart alignment. When this occurs, our fear becomes our truth. Of course, it's not the absolute truth. But it becomes our truth, and it influences everything we do, say, and feel. Thereby our fearful thoughts, beliefs, and actions cause us to actually attract the outcome that we are in fact afraid of. When someone tells me, "I was afraid of that," I know what they have been thinking.

Once we are free of this dynamic, we can be more persuasive, bold, and powerful. How we feel and think dictates how we speak, act, behave, and lead others, which in turn drives our outcomes. **If you want to change how you feel, then take action to change what you think.**

Epicurus, in the third century BCE, pointed out that humans live under two masters: the pursuit of pleasure and the desire to avoid pain. Sigmund Freud expanded on the topic with the principle by adding in the id, our animalistic force buried deep inside us all that seeks immediate gratification (also called lizard brain).

As toddlers, our id runs the show. If we want it, we grab it. A thirsty toddler will grab your glass off the coffee table and take a drink. But we eventually develop the ego, which helps us learn to act on what is appropriate in a given setting. At this point we become aware of others in our world, that life is not just about us. It is the development of the ego and the awareness that prevents us from taking a swig from our boss's water bottle.

In the pleasure and pain equation, it is my opinion that pain wins. Avoiding pain is often a far more powerful reaction than pursing pleasure. For example, a mature human being faced with a balanced decision between the pursuit of grand pleasure versus the fear of great pain will most likely listen to their fear to avoid pain, especially when the pursuit of pleasure involves the risk of pain. The same is true when the desire for pleasure is small, but the fear of pain is also small; listening to fear wins.

Let's say you have been on the job for some time, and you feel you have performed well. You have noticed others getting a raise, and you think you deserve one also. Do you ask for a raise and enjoy the pleasure of additional income, or do you listen to your fear of being turned down and risk both self-esteem and possibly damage to your relationship with your boss?

Most people do not ask for a raise even if they think it is deserved. Rest easy as you read this. I am going to show you how to change the leverage power in your choices, after you have weighed carefully the risk/reward decision. I will show you how to find the power, after careful evaluation, to choose progress and success even in the face of fear.

Consider this scenario: You are in a meeting. You see a problem with the plan that has been pitched and is about to be adopted. Should you raise your hand and critique the basic idea or strategy and offer a better solution? Yes. But you perceive that the CEO is already enrolled in the idea as presented. If you disagree, you could lose political capital with your peers and boss. But you work in a publicly traded company, and you have stock options. A wrong decision could cause a decrease in the stock price, which affects you personally.

What do you do?

Seeking pleasure would cause you to find your courage and voice your objection and offer improvements. But speaking your new and maybe unpopular idea might cost you a promotion plus the retribution from the colleague who authored the original idea. You fear that you might miss your bonus because you were not a team player.

Depending on the social and cultural norms in the organization and how the majority of the vote count looks at the moment, you will often default to your fear and choose not to voice your concern or offer your new idea.

Let's make this more relevant and simpler. How likely are you to raise your hand and speak in a meeting before knowing how your comments will be received? During any business meeting, 80 percent of the people never offer their opinions until asked. We find it hard to speak up because of fear, even when there is no evidence that fear is justified.

In the final analysis, fear causes us to play small in life. Even though listening to our fear is often rationalized as wisdom, it is really the quiet subconscious ego urging us to avoid pain. The ego wins by writing and repeating unfounded stories that make it easy not to risk. When this happens day after day, we stop being bold, which unfortunately means that we stop making a powerful difference. Somehow this turns into an autopilot response to opportunity, and we can become people who are called risk averse in general. Others may have modeled their life and thinking and are seen as risk takers.

Along the way, our passion gets extinguished. Our creativity subsides, and we simply choose to play it safe, living out our lives on autopilot, just standing around waiting to see if we get to win. Our wisdom so often tells us no, while our naiveté would have said why not? Let's go for it. What do you think? How does this show up in your life?

It's no wonder the military drafts eighteen-year-olds. Logically you would think they would want thirty-year-olds. A mature soldier combines wisdom with experience and thus is capable of making better decisions. But the military knows that less experience equals more fearlessness. And that's what they need.

As we reach our career stride and get older, we just seem to be prone to listening to our fear and obeying its prompting more and more. So we take fewer risks as we get older, even though the risks are actually less risky *because* we have gained wisdom and maturity. Maturity and experience actually set us up with greater chances for success. Ironically, by the time we are finally equipped to make better decisions, we actually stop risking as much as we did when we were young and naive.

At twenty-something years old, the average guy would more readily embrace any blind date as an adventure to see what could happen. At thirty-five, that same guy has become much more selective and cautious because he has experienced one too many disastrous dates. Pain has made him cautious.

As we get older, we become more skeptical. On the one hand, we protect ourselves from pain, but on the other, we limit our options and the possibility of finding true love. Same for friendships and relationships. At age sixty-five, I find it more difficult to make new friends.

It pains me to watch this natural dynamic unfold in all of us. When we are young and dumb, we live out full lives fraught with glory, pain, and adventure. When we are older, we live more peaceful, guarded, and smaller lives. But this occurs at a time when we are actually more capable of living full and successful lives due to our wisdom.

THE WALKING DEAD

After four decades of intense research and work with leaders in the business world, and over two decades of being invited behind closed doors into the deepest places of people's emotional lives as a coach, I clearly see that there are big missing pieces in their lives.

Sure, they feel safer (they think) and more secure. But the majority of my clients age forty and above are living in somewhat of a trance, like on autopilot, unaware they are driven by subtle fear. Often, they don't risk much, but they don't gain much either. They don't really feel alive any longer. They work hard but take no big risks and thus have little chance for glory. They certainly don't experience adventure and, as a result, have little possibility for massive success.

We can't expect big rewards by playing small. If they were honest, many would admit that this insulated and stale life is barely worth living.

When I see the winter of my life coming at me like a storm, I want to redeem the time—*carpe diem*. I want to live out the rest of my days like a supernova, not like a flickering candle that goes out without being noticed. I want my life to matter in this world. How about you? Regardless how old or young you are, the end will come sooner than you think.

Look at your life today. Are you living a life that you feel represents your true potential? If not, what are you waiting for? Life will not get easier; you just get stronger. Are you waiting for your ship to come in? Ships don't come into port to pick up one person. You have to dive off the dock and swim out to it.

When I write about fear, please understand I am not referencing a heightened state that causes your palms to sweat or creates a knot in your stomach. The fear I am referring to here is subtle fear. This kind of fear is not intense enough for you to physically feel its presence, but it is still there behind the scenes of your conscious mind, steering your ship. Subtle fear is that self-questioning thought that makes you pause instead of going after what you want.

It's much like the time Dorothy meets the great wizard, Oz. While the loud deep voice pontificates, Toto pulls away the curtain at the side of the stage to reveal a frantic little man working levers to make the scene appear grand.

"Pay no attention to the man behind the curtain. I am the great and powerful Wizard of Oz." Your ego says that too. "I am not afraid. I am just using my head and being careful. Listen to my wisdom. I am just trying to keep you safe from what obviously will become troubling to you. You are not stupid. Look at the facts I have presented to you."

But this wisdom, even though it's based on historical evidence, is constructed to make you fearful and to avoid risk at all cost, even at the expense of glory and success. The ego is quietly urging: "I am not afraid. I am just using my head." Maybe you should use your experience and maturity to prevent you from acting on an opportunity, but maybe, just maybe, you should move forward.

Look at just the facts, not your stories in your head. When you do, you will often discover that the worst thing that could happen is that you hear someone say no. If that's the total sum of your risk, then maybe you can decide to just go for it.

The tragic principle of success is that people who succeed the most have learned to endure pain. They know that pain is a natural part of life, and meant to be embraced, because pain is the catalyst for growth and learning. I am going to use a biblical principle, which was intended for a totally different reason but appropriate here: "More than that, we rejoice in our sufferings, knowing that suffering produces endurance, and endurance produces character, and character produces hope" (Romans 5:34).

Gary was the CEO of a company that failed miserably, but it wasn't his fault. Gary's first failure was the direct result of an overly greedy board of directors. The board voted to turn down a $360-million merger offer for the company because they wanted more. In hindsight that $360M was a generous offer for a $40M revenue company. Gary and the entire executive team fully supported the sale of the company because they needed the huge influx of money as well as a big partner to take the company to the next level. But the board said no because they wanted to hold out for an even bigger offer.

One thing led to another, and quickly word got out that the company was on the market. It is a principle that when someone makes an offer to buy your company, the board would like to see who else might want to buy you. The myth is that such buzz creates a feeding frenzy that dibs up the ultimate price of the company. But one thing you need to know is that companies are bought, not sold. If I want to sell you my car, one of your first questions should be why? If the car is so nice, why would I sell it? If your company is so great, why would you not believe in your future and build up the company yourself? Why do you want out?

Gary was not done yet. He had founded a second company, which was a high-tech start-up based on cool technology built for the enterprise space. His company was ahead of its time in cloud technology, so the market had not quite formulated the problem for Gary's solution. Gary and his team soon realized they were just a couple years ahead of the broad market adoption of the cloud. This understandably delayed rapid sales growth.

All the prospects said, "I love your solution, and want it, but we are just not ready to switch to the cloud, which means I can't use your fantastic solution."

After five years, the company had raised three rounds of financing. In the venture world, it was a play that was getting old. The new investors were getting anxious to do an M/A and get out for their sake, even if it was not in the company's best interest. With the company's revenue of about $40M, it was not going to be an IPO play.

All of a sudden Gary remembered the history of his first company. He was now even more fearful of the board of directors and their goals, which finally led him to a place where he became emotionally resigned. Right after every coaching session with me, he was fine. But in a couple of days, no matter how much I tried, subtle fear would take over. All the conversations in the executive team were about mitigating risk, developing and working on a plan B, and then a plan C. The executive team lost sight of the vision and potential of the company. They were constantly in plan B and C discussions.

Because fear is contagious, especially when the CEO has a case of it, the team became scared. Executives began to quietly update their resumes. The team, prospective buyers, and customers could smell the fear a mile away. In the end, the company did do an M/A to a big player in the market, but Gary could not say it was a big payday. I deeply love him. It saddens me deeply that he didn't get his deserved big payday. He accidentally sourced into reality what he was most afraid of. This company was finally acquired by a huge tech company, but for a very modest price.

PLAYING SAFE IS THE MOST DANGEROUS WAY TO PLAY

The first step to overcoming fear is admitting you have it. Pride and ego don't want you to admit or acknowledge that you have subtle fear. The ego says, "If you admit even to yourself that you are afraid, things will get worse and you will be even more afraid." The ego uses fear to keep you from even examining why you're afraid. Which clearly does not work. Only when we recognize and admit a problem do we have a chance to fix it. I think this is crazy. Our fear of looking fearful to others prevents us from being honest with ourselves in analyzing if we are fearful.

Hidden and unchecked fear is a self-fulfilling prophecy. Our fear makes us play small. Yet ironically, playing small is always the most dangerous way to play. When you play small, your company does nothing bold. You never get noticed. You just stand there swinging it out toe-to-toe in the fight against an equal rival, where nobody wins. It takes a toll on money, time of opportunity, and lost passion and energy. Playing safe is the best way to ultimately fail. *Now if you run a nuclear power plant, forget what I just said.*

Second, remember that most fears are completely unfounded. About 90 percent of what we are afraid of never comes to pass. Let the facts help you rise above your fabricated stories of what might happen.

Then, third, master mindfulness. This is living in the present moment. In this moment, there is nothing to be afraid of. Fear can only live in the place called the future. So bring your mind's attention to the here and now.

Let me prove it to you right now. Right now, in this moment, *this moment*, what do you have to fear in this moment? The answer is nothing. Anything you came up with deals with fifteen minutes from now, later today, tomorrow, or in the weeks to come. It's great to take 10 percent of your time to strategize about the future. This is necessary. But then come back to live and act in the present moment 90 percent of the day.

I want deep and meaningful relationships not only in business but in every area of my life. I know that I have to be authentic and vulnerable with people in order to create these relationships. But even the thought of vulnerability causes fear.

Here is what playing it safe and staying small because of subtle fear looks like in our day-to-day life. I want to shoot myself when I hear conversations like this in line at Starbucks:

"How are you, Bill?

"I'm fine. Things are good. How's the family?"

"Family's good. How's work going?"

"Eh, you know, good days and bad days. How about you, Pete?"

"I'm good. Family is good. Kelly started third grade."

"How's the job?"

"Oh, you know, it's fine."

"Nice to have the rain stop and see some sun, huh?"

"Yeah, but I've got to catch a flight to New York and be gone most of the week so I'll miss it. Have to go to a corporate quarterly review."

"Hey, Pete, let's get together and have coffee when I come back."

"Okay. Why? Is everything okay, Bill?"

"Of course, just thought we could get together and catch up."

"Okay. I'll call you next week."

Why get together again? What a waste of oxygen and time to meet again for the same shallow conversation. How many times do you leave a conversation with someone only to feel empty inside? Like there was no substance, no new understanding, and no new deeper connection realized? I call it a Facebook conversation, where we hide behind our success mask and pretend that life is just fine. Often, we point out anything good we can so we can appear to be in a happy place. We crave love and acceptance from others, but to be honest, we think this deeper discussion might make us look bad, and we might lose even this shallow acquaintance.

The truth of the matter is quite opposite. When we get real, authentic, honest, and vulnerable, people want to connect with us even deeper.

Here is the real communication I wish everyone could have, but don't because of the fear of what others might think:

"Hey, Bill, it's good to see you. How are you?"

"Okay, I guess. I'm bored, I feel like I am just cruising through life, and I am feeling a little dead inside. My company seems to have just stalled out and the thrill is gone."

"I get what you are saying. I sometimes fight regrets that I should have done this or that years ago. I'd like to get together and talk. I kinda need a friend. I need to get out of this funk."

"I know what you mean. It feels like I'm hitting a brick wall in my career, and I don't get enough time at home anymore. It feels like my life is running me, instead of me running my life."

"I feel you brother."

"Hey, you got time to grab a cup of coffee now?"

Now I admit we can't have those vulnerable conversations with the acquaintances we run into at Starbucks. It just wouldn't be wise. Acquaintances haven't become close enough to share that kind of vulnerability. But do we ever call up a best friend and have that kind of conversation? Heck no. We don't even want our best friend to think less of us. We think, "Heck, I am afraid I would scare off my best friend. Have you seen his Facebook page? His life is perfect."

BELIEVE IN COURAGE AND FOCUS ON THE MISSION

Most of us believe that courage is a feeling that few people have—a trait that enables them to do bold acts in the face of danger. We somehow think these people are just naturally courageous. In some rare cases that may be true. But courage is often nothing more than a decision made in the face of fear, to say or do something worthwhile.

Most often people do courageous things despite feeling fearful. Courage is not just a feeling; it's a decision in the face of fear. Courage is doing the hard task in the face of your fear, not in the absence of it. The absence of fear can be just plain stupidity.

Brené Brown describes courage as a heart word. The root of the word *courage* is *cor*—the Latin word for *heart*. In one of its earliest forms, the word *courage* meant "to speak one's mind by telling all one's heart." Over time, this definition has changed, and, today, we typically associate courage with heroic and brave deeds. But in my opinion, today's definition fails to recognize the inner strength and level of commitment required for us to actually speak honestly and openly about who we are and about our experiences—good and bad. Speaking from our hearts is what I think of as ordinary courage. And this kind of courage can be deployed each and every day.

My belief of courage is that it is a worthwhile prompting to say or do something that will put myself at risk, but I do it anyway. In order for me to do this, my self-esteem must be high enough that I would be willing to take a hit if the situation doesn't turn out well.

Over the last nineteen years I have worked with one CEO, off and on, at two different companies. Phillip is one of the most honest men I know. He is the perfect example of courage and has the ability to speak from the heart.

During one session he asked me about the work and progress I was having with his executives. It was a fair question. But he was pacing the floor, looking around, yet in control and confident. But I was there for his and my session, not just to download my work with his team. It felt like an avoidance of taking on the real work between us as coach and CEO. This time I didn't answer his question. Instead I looked up and paused, then I lovingly asked him, "What are you afraid of?"

He looked down, walked over to the chair in front of me, sat down, and said, "I'm afraid of what the board is thinking and will do in light of our recent setback. I am concerned about the liquidity event before we know how it will turn out. I am afraid that the team is not ready for the rigorous accountability of being a public company."

We processed each one of his concerns and had a fruitful meeting. He faced his fear.

When I called him out from autopilot and got real, he had the courage to wade in and admit his fear. He was honest and vulnerable. And because of his courage, we connected and got some real work done, with some big breakthroughs and strategies. This is what makes him an effective CEO.

Another contributor to courage is a strong belief in your mission. This belief needs to permeate your heart to the point that your mission actually owns you. Your mission is stronger than your self-esteem. You serve the mission, not yourself.

We find this trait in the story of Desmond Doss, which was portrayed in the true story of *Hacksaw Ridge*. In the movie Desmond was actually ridiculed by his teammates, and physically beaten for his conscientious objector choice. He wanted to be a medic and save lives, not take them. As you see in his story, despite being hated by his comrades, he single-handedly saved seventy-five lives during the battle of Okinawa. Alone, through the night, Desmond retrieved the wounded and attended to them, finally lowering each one over a cliff to safety using a rope harness he created.

After that battle every man revered Desmond for his courage. Once thought of as an incredible coward, he was seen as a courageously true hero. Desmond is an example of a man whose mission was larger than himself and kept him going. He is a fantastic example of courage with no one having his back. Courage is usually a lonely path.

The third catalyst for courage is passion. We are going to get into this in detail a little later. But suffice it to say that if you want something with passion, that desire creates a drive larger than anything else in the world, and in that drive, you will find courage. You become bold. You don't care if there is any support around you or your idea. You become a maniac on a mission, a zealot. When you are full of passion to the point of commitment, it's really hard to fail.

A critical element necessary for any of the paths to courage is the element of strong self-love and healthy self-esteem. Good self-esteem helps us to look at our lives and become willing to reconcile our past. When we are reconciled with our past, it can't take us down any longer.

Because of fear, we are not usually willing to even look at or evaluate our self-esteem. We are not willing to admit that our self-esteem is not strong enough to take risks of courage to say or do what we really want. The real root of courage starts with an honest look at ourselves and a commitment to clean up our past, so we can finally love ourselves.

Who am I to me? What do I stand for? Am I proud of the man or woman I am and am becoming? Am I living a life that is congruent to my beliefs and standards? Am I proud of me, in a most humble way? And have I reconciled myself with my past by cleaning up any wrongdoing on my part with others, so I can feel good about myself?

All success—whether it is with my self-esteem, my family, friends, career, or even hobbies—is an inside job. External success always begins in my heart and then shows up as fruit or a reality externally in my career traction, or in the level of intimacy in all my relationships.

The birth of courage is found in the willingness to be honest—with myself first. Socrates nailed it when he said, "To know thyself is the beginning of wisdom." To deeply look into our souls and be honest with what we see is really scary. But it is the foundational work we all get to do in order to grow and be free of the past.

Without this honest examination and admission to self, we cannot change, because we never see the need for change. Yet we feel unsatisfied. How do we dance this dance of denial, stuffing down emotions, avoiding the truth of self? We write stories that we think justify and rationalize our actions and beliefs. In more extreme cases we turn to drugs, alcohol, gambling, porn, shopping, or power tripping as coping mechanisms. But since everybody around us is living out lives in quiet desperation, we have come to believe that this is the norm. How sad.

Many times, a fearful CEO will blame the board for their lack of support. Or they will be angry at their executive team that they are not making a commitment to execution. But it's up to the CEO to lead the board and the executive team. If something is not working in the company, there is no one else to blame but you. You are the CEO, and you are responsible for creating alignment and commitment to execution traction. Fear creates the desire for blaming and feeling somewhat like a victim. Which never ends well. Courage takes responsibility for everything around you.

If we truly want a life worth living, it takes only a moderate amount of courage to be honest with yourself, and then the willingness to take action to admit our faults to those we have harmed, so we can love ourselves again. If you find yourself still reluctant to do this, find your best friend, brother, sister, or minister to share your honest heart with. Courage is like a muscle; it can be strengthened and can grow with practice. The main point is to start building courage, start with working on yourself. Fall in love with you in a healthy way. Live with integrity and honesty.

The more you love yourself, the more you will naturally feel like saying, "I am pretty good. I feel whole and complete. How are you? How can I be there for you?" When you are not preoccupied with your own life, you'll notice opportunities where you can be present for others. This is a necessary ingredient to empowering all relationships with friends and family and in the workplace. BTW, this selfless attitude is critical to leadership.

As a leader, there is something incredibly powerful when you look your direct report in the eye and say, "I completely believe in you." But if you say this, you must mean it. If you can't say it, why are they still employed by you? Why not replace them today?

Leadership is not about you. It's about them. Can you look your employee or direct report in the eye and see they are already successful, and if they aren't, what can you do to inspire, lead, encourage, hold them by the hand, anything you can think of to take responsibility for their success?

After you have done this, and they are still not successful, then out of love you need to let them go. Why keep them prisoner in a job that you both know they are not winning at? If you love them, let them go. Do you have the courage to let them go? If not now, then when? Why will tomorrow be a better time?

When you show your team you are in complete support of them because you believe in them, they will rarely disappoint you. And if they do, dive in and help them. If that doesn't work, then replace them from a place of love, with a clear conscience. Let them see you are completely behind them. If your team authentically believes that you believe in them, they will knock your socks off. When they feel this kind of loving support—along with your courage to hold their feet to the fire—they will focus on meeting their deadlines because they do not want to disappoint you. When they watch you take bold action to let someone go, who needs to leave, they will respect you deeply.

TAKEAWAYS

- Fear is our ally and our nemesis. It protects us from real world danger, but it also causes us to hesitate and play small. This is a killer for a leader.
- More often than not, anger is not the root emotion. It is fear that causes anger. So we get to attack the root cause of fear, not the symptom of anger.
- Fear naturally wins over passion in the unexamined life.
- As we get older, we have more experience and tend to listen to our fear more than when we are young.
- Fear is a self-fulfilling prophecy. The most dangerous way to play at life is often to play it safe.
- When you bring your awareness to the present moment through mindfulness, fear vanishes.
- Fear keeps us in shallow conversations, which prevents real human connection.

- Remembering and focusing on your mission takes fear away because it takes your awareness away from self.
- Passion is the great antithesis of fear. Passion is like cold water on a hot fire.
- The birthplace of courage is found in the bowels of self-honesty.

7

THE BLAME GAME

Would you say that our country is divided in almost every way possible? If you listen to the news for just a moment, you hear everyone blaming someone for everything. Blame is a form of self-righteousness. And it's easy.

Blame artificially helps us cope with frustration. That's like taking an opioid for the pain, rather than fixing what ails us. Blame also leads us to build anger, which robs us of our peace. Today it seems like everyone is willing to trade their peace for blaming and being right about their righteous ideologies. Rather than doing the hard work of being a solution to any problem, it's just so easy to fold our arms in disgust and blame someone. Of course, the obvious problem with blame is that with it, nothing can get better. Nothing.

So here's the bad news. There is no one external to blame. Blame is the natural and easy response to emotional pain, expressed as anger.

Fear is usually seen as anger. There are usually two causes of fear. One is not getting what I want. And the other is the fear of losing what I've got.

If I don't get what I want, or if I lose what I've got, then I feel emotional pain.

"I want Debbie to love me, and she doesn't." That's a simple example of not getting what I want, as unrequited love.

"Debbie and I have been together for some time, and she just left me." That's an example of losing what I had.

Replace the name Debbie with a promotion, or a job, a friend, a new car, or my kid getting a D on their report card. Pain says, "This hurts. I don't want to accept that the pain I feel has anything to do with me, my attitudes, or expectations. I want to blame someone else for causing me this pain. It has to be someone's fault, because it hurts, and I don't want to look inside."

But the problem with this solution is that we don't change anyone or anything.

One of the hardest principles I learned was something someone told me over a decade ago. "If you want freedom of choice, then take the pill of responsibility for everything in your life."

Yes, embrace that you are exactly where you are in life because of the choices you have made. This includes marriage, job, friends, or addictions. You see when I choose the hard path of responsibility, rather than the easy path of blame, then I am only free to change what disturbs me. Because I can change me, I can't change anyone else.

WHO'S TO BLAME?

I was the president of a nonprofit called Project Heart. We worked with addicts and alcoholics who were convicted of crimes and sent to jail. We deployed the principles outlined in this book—the principles of love, acceptance, relationships full of mutual support, making amends, taking responsibility for our lives, and seeking help from a power greater than ourselves.

Larry Hensley was probably thirty-five years old, 6 feet 3, and 220 pounds of muscle. He had just been paroled from Folsom Prison. Surprisingly, he had the warmest and most loving heart. Every time I saw him, he would lean close, look me in the eyes, and make me feel he was excited to see me again. He proclaimed that he was absolutely committed to never doing drugs again and wanted to build a great life for himself. I know people, and I believed him.

He and I immediately connected and grew close. He attended all our meetings regularly and engaged in discussions and offered help to others. I saw something in him that was real promise due to his willingness to do whatever was needed to be a loving, contributing member of society. He had a true desire for human connection. I even took him to Carson City, Nevada, with a group for three days of training to learn about mentoring others. He wanted to reach back and make a difference for those who were also trying to get their lives together.

I happened to hear him say a couple of times how much he liked my Rocky Boots. So I found out his shoe size and ordered him a pair. When they arrived, I called him and said, "I need a little help, could you drop by my house for a few minutes?" I didn't explain what kind of help I needed.

He said, "Sure, I get off work at five. I could come over right after work." When he arrived, I asked him into the house saying I wanted to show him my new boots. He told me how cool they looked. And I could see an innocent envy in his eyes. He probably thought that I had forgotten how he had complemented me for my boots previously, so it probably felt a little cruel.

I said, "But I have a problem. These are size eleven and a half, and I only wear a ten and a half. Hey, they might fit you. Here try them on." In that moment he realized that they were a gift all along. With tears in his eyes he gave me a big bear hug and genuinely thanked me. Of course, I received far more satisfaction from his happiness than I ever did from a new pair of boots for myself.

Over time, he secured a good job, got busy, and had a new girlfriend. So I didn't see him quite so often. So about six months ago he went dark. I called and left messages, but he never called back. I suspected that he had fallen back into drugs again. I would hear from others in our program that they had seen him, and he wasn't doing well. But no one knew where Larry was. Then I got the call. While out having dinner with a couple of people, Larry went to the restaurant's bathroom. After being gone too long, his friends checked on him, only to discover him on the toilet, with a needle in his arm, dead. No one could revive him. Even as I write this, my heart breaks all over again.

Who is to blame for Larry's passing? I am hurting, and I need to find someone to blame. Is it the drug lab in some trailer kitchen somewhere deep in the mountains? Is it the dealer who sold him the drugs, and while making a profit killed my friend? Is it the drug enforcement police for not shutting down the lab and arresting the dealer? Is it the prison system for not rehabilitating him while he was in prison for three years? Is it his parents for not loving him enough? Is it me for failing to track him down and forcing him into rehab? Is it our very society that doesn't make all of us feel loved enough, so we don't need to mask our pain with drugs?

None of these are to blame.

I don't understand how this can happen every day in America. Because I don't understand, I need to make sense of my pain and find someone to blame. But what if there is no real explanation at all? What if this is life? What if everything I knew about Larry was accurately the truth. For whatever reason, he overdosed and died. I will never understand. I don't have to create a reason why he died so I can blame someone. I can discipline myself to accept that there are things I may never understand. In this way, I can grieve and let him go.

Now acceptance that life includes pain does not mean that we stop trying to fix all those problems I just outlined, but it may mean that I get to accept that bad things happen, and I can't fix many of them. I get to try though. I get to embrace life on life's terms, instead of expecting life to meet me on mine.

When the Larrys of this life die, or your spouse leaves you, or you get fired, and you feel deep and profound pain, maybe acceptance of the facts is the only profitable, yet painful answer. Pain is a part of life. Period. But I don't have to find someone to blame. I don't have to pick up a drug or a drink to smother the pain. Maybe I am just supposed to feel the pain and reach out to friends and loved ones and grieve while being held by someone I love and trust. No one has ever died from feeling a feeling. What kills us are the things that we do in pain, or the things we use to cope with the fear and pain; but feelings alone will not cause death.

This is your chance to stop blaming everyone, anyone. Look inside and just feel what you feel. Share your pain with someone. If you keep it bottled up inside, it will eat you alive and haunt you forever. Life is meant to be a shared experience. We are hardwired to love and be loved. We are genetically driven to be in a tribe. When we get in the way of experiencing our emotions fully, life begins to unravel, and we often resort to drugs, alcohol, shopping, pornography, eating, materialism, and more to numb the pain we never acknowledge. The more than 200 different 12-step programs in the world can't be wrong.

I want you to be emotionally free. Because I covet peace. That means not collecting emotional baggage, accepting life on life's terms, sharing your pain as a way to cope, ridding yourself of resentments, and letting go of bitterness. When you are emotionally free, love and passion and creativity can more easily flow to the surface of your mind, heart, and life.

TAKEAWAYS

- Blame is a natural response to pain. It's easy, everywhere, and doesn't help a thing.
- Fear causes anger, and anger causes blame.
- Fear is usually based on two things. Fear of losing what I have, or not getting what I want.

- The opposite of blame is responsibility. I am where I am because of some choice I made along life's path.
- Responsibility brings choice to your doorstep while blame is a dead-end street.
- I can change me. I can't change anyone else.
- Sometimes bad things happen, and I just get to be with it, like losing Larry. Feelings are meant to be felt, not diverted onto someone else.

8

REWRITE THE STORIES IN YOUR HEAD

We create stories in our head all the time, about everything. Now is the time to rewrite them because they are not serving you anymore. Most of the stories we write are deeply influenced by what has happened to us in the past. The more wounds and resentments we have in our past, the more stories we write in our minds about how things are likely to not turn out well in our future.

Here's the point: Most of our lives are driven by our looking at life through the lens of our past. Something happens around you today. Often this new situation reminds you of something similar in the past. The event can bring up a painful memory of what happened and how it turned out then.

Instead of seeing the new event as new, it's easy to project the same negative outcome from this new event. This is just the ego trying to warn you that the sky may be falling all over again, and urge you to retreat to safety. And this feels justified because we see it as wisdom. But this thinking is so limiting. This is a new event, and it may be an opportunity we could miss because of the influence of looking at today through the lens of the past.

I am going to call you a name right now. Check to see if what I am about to write deeply offends you. "You are a dirty rotten bank robber."

Are you offended? Of course not. Why? Because you know there is absolutely no truth in the statement. There is no past guilt, wounds, or shame there because you never robbed a bank.

But what if I called you a name that indeed resonated with your past? Let's say you used to tell a lie now and then, and I called you a liar?

Or if you tended to be a procrastinator and were always late for meetings and I called you a slacker. How would that feel? Oh, that's a different story. When you have unresolved guilt or shame around something in your past, and I make a comment that nicks a vein of truth in you, it is natural to become hurt and offended.

We only get angry when someone does or says something that brings up some small hidden truth that we want to deny. Many of the things that really bother us in life are rooted in some form of hidden truth in our past. Here is a side note we love to deny. If someone does or says something that really bothers you, often you will find some element of their behavior in you.

Here is a personal example: I hate it when someone is late for a meeting with me. When I look deeply inside myself, I discover I am annoyed at their tardiness because it feels like disrespect. That acknowledged, the next question is, why do I need the validation of their timeliness to assure their respect for me? Where is the root wound that causes me to think people don't respect me?

My annoyance is rooted in an event that happened years ago when someone was late and effectively told me, "You are not that important, and I will arrive when I want to." That event hurt. I immediately wrote a story that as far as they were concerned, I was a person who is not worthy of respect. And instead of finding out what was going on in their life that caused them to hurt me, I just nursed the anger and the hurt and used it to create a story that said, "I am worthy of respect, and I will demand that you show up supporting that belief." Of course when someone is late to a meeting with me, it doesn't mean they don't respect me. But without examination, I would have never seen this playing out in my life.

The key element here is to be really honest with ourselves and clean up our past. Remember, Socrates: "The unexamined life is not worth living." When we get hurt or offended, dig and find out the root cause that surfaced to cause your emotional reaction. When we apologize for something we do or say, the wound or guilt disappears. If someone says something that hurts to hear, we get to look at why it hurts. There may be some element of truth to it; otherwise, it would be like comparing you to John Dillinger, and since you haven't robbed a bank, ever, you laugh at the comment.

When we begin to see what is in the background leading us to feel what we feel, we can rewrite the story and have future instances that won't bring up the emotions of the past quite so easily. This is living a life that seeks freedom from the power of the past.

One significant way to become whole and complete about your past is to examine every instance that shows up today to hurt you and find the past example that is the original event. Then look at the black and white of the original event. You will often discover that the original event was not cause for a moment of hurt, guilt, or shame but was, instead, a rough emotional moment for the person who spoke those harsh words to you.

In this way, you can rewrite the original story, thus unleashing freedom from an autopilot reaction today. If you happen to look back and see that you were at fault for some part of the hurtful experience, then we get the choice to go back to that person and make amends. When you clean up your side of the street, then the guilt and shame disappear.

When you are whole and complete, you show up to the world with emotional maturity, security, and assurance, and always respond with grace under pressure so no one can knock you off center. In this case, you can seek out the basis of any problem without getting distracted by pain, anger, and blame. These are signs of a solid leader.

A SELF-FULFILLING PROPHECY

My client Ted was the VP of sales. When we meet, he was worked up about missing this quarter's sales numbers. But the quarter was not over yet. In fact, there were still two weeks to go. He spoke of missing the number as a prophetic reality. He was fearful of what the CEO was going to think and say when he missed the numbers. He was worried about the judgment from his peers in the organization. He was troubled by how he was going to lead the team after the miss and still keep them inspired for the next quarter.

He was not even aware that he was angry. He feared that this miss would be a direct hit to his self-esteem.

You see, Ted viewed himself as a man who always hit his numbers. Ted saw himself as a winner, and this prophetic future was not aligned with his self-image. His thoughts of the missed quarter had been churning in his mind for over a month. Long enough that the story had taken up residence in his head and was affecting his emotions.

Now that the thinking and the feeling were in alignment and both agreed that, yes, he would miss his sales target, he was resigned to a prophecy of his own making. Ted's conversations were all about how we were going to manage the miss. Insight and passion to find creative ways to make up the shortfall in revenue had long passed. Now that he was already embracing the bad news, he was crafting the story for his CEO. This made him subtly fearful.

When Ted met with the CEO, he reeked of fear. Therefore, the CEO started writing stories in his mind:

- There is going to be a miss in the revenue this quarter.
- I now have to tell the board about the miss.
- Ted is scared, which dents the CEO's confidence.
- How can Ted go out next quarter and passionately and creatively make up for this quarter's loss, so we can hit the annual projection?

- In Ted's state of fear, he has answers as to why we missed, but no creative plan on how we are going to excel going forward. His answer seems to be "work harder."
- Now the contagion of fear is planted a little bit in the CEO. The rest of the VPs know about the imminent failure and so the fear is becoming viral.

As his coach, I could smell the fear. It was thick in the air. I decided to do my storytelling exercise.

I artificially contorted my face to make it appear disgusted, then slammed my open hand on the table as I leaned forward to stare him in the eye. Ted stared back with no response. After the echo of the desk slap subsided, I relaxed my features and asked, "Tell me what you feel just happened when I slammed my hand on the table."

Ted responded, "Well it looks like you are frustrated with me. I guess you are going to tell me how I am wrong about something. It looks like you are angry."

I said, "Nope. I am actually very happy, contented, and peaceful this morning. In fact, the only feeling I have is one of gratitude because I get to spend the morning with you. All I did was just contort my face with a look of anger and slammed my hand on the table. There was absolutely no intent behind it at all. I just wanted to show you how you and I, and the rest of the world, make up stories about everything. There was no ill feeling of any kind in my heart at that moment. It was just a fabricated exercise, and I was acting."

But I said, "Do you see how you created a strong story about what you think I did and what I must be feeling? Can you see that you might just be wrong about many of the stories you write in your head?"

In other words, I was saying to Ted, you may not be wrong about the event, but you may often be wrong about why it happened. Facts are facts and should be embraced and accepted. It's the fabricated stories about why it happened and what it means that is tripping you up.

You think that you will miss this quarter's revenue goal, and you have thought it long enough that it has driven you to believe you will miss.

When your head and your heart agree on something, it becomes your truth, and that dramatically affects your words and actions. Missing this quarter's sales may not be true at all, but at this point, it doesn't matter because you will be acting on your truth of your story. The quarter has two more weeks to go, yet you've already quit.

In our discussion, I pointed out a principle that I really didn't want him to miss: Pain and suffering do not come from the event of missing the quarter. Missing the quarter is just missing the quarter. The pain manifests in the stories that we fabricate about missing the quarter where all the pain and suffering are embedded. The negative story that he has written will become a self-fulfilling prophecy for him if he continues to embrace his story as the truth.

What's at play here is just the ego thinking that if it gets you to write a failed prophetic outcome, you could avoid the tragic pain of sudden disappointment. It wants you to embrace the failure today, so you can make excuses, point a finger of blame, or get the CEO to be prepared that the quarter will be missed. The ego thinks it is creating a soft landing for a failure that may come.

The painful event of missing the quarter might be painful during the last night of the quarter, but not for much longer than that. Like I told Ted, he had already suffered for over a month that he might miss the quarter. And he could feel guilty and fearful for the whole next quarter about missing the next, which can become a self-fulfilling prophecy.

I suggested, "How about you just wait until 6:00 p.m. on the last day of the quarter to see if you missed? Then feel bad. But play all out from this moment until that time. If you miss the quarter, you will have the satisfaction that you played all out until the quarter was over. Then if you miss, you can feel badly for one night, and then address the new quarter fresh like a brand-new quarter, which it will be."

This was difficult work for Ted. Once a story is written, and a subsequent emotion is experienced based on the fabricated story, it is difficult to change. If Ted and I are not careful, Ted's story, and the self-fulfilling prophecy will begin to alter his own self-image to match the story he created. He could very well start telling himself that he is not as good as he thought he was, and that missing the revenue goal may become a more frequent event. He can become a person who begins to question whether he has what it takes or not. Ted could bring out his resume and freshen it up, because his own story has convinced him he needs to pursue another opportunity. Ted could begin telling himself a story about why it's time to leave the company.

But Ted can catch himself early in this negative loop and choose to write a different, more empowering story.

REWRITE THE STORY TO CHANGE YOUR LIFE

Understand that you have a free will to write and embrace any story you choose. Why not write and tell yourself a story of success and power and victory? Both the good and bad stories are not steeped in prophetic fact. Why not choose one that leads you to power? And whatever story you write and tell yourself, you will begin believing and feeling that it's true. By carefully choosing the story you write on purpose, you are taking control of your life. But it all begins by seeing the distinction that your stories are a choice, your choice. They don't have to be some prophetic destiny filled with gloom.

Almost all of humanity is not even aware that they are sitting in the bleachers reporting on the story of their life, when, all along, they could be playing on the field, writing the story of a grand life. We are really the authors of our story, and our life. We can create and be anything we want. If you doubt that last sentence because you are afraid to believe, where's the evidence? Prove to me that you can't do your next great thing.

Another underlying reason we write stories all the time is based on our deep desire for certainty. We believe that certainty will make us feel secure. We feel we need to make sense out of everything, every instance, every event of our life. If we don't understand the meaning of what's going on at any given moment, we really get scared. Since we can't see the real truth of the *why* of every word spoken or action taken, we create and write a story to fill in the blanks between the points of data. We feel that this will create an understanding of what's going to happen. And we all want to know what's going to happen next. And none of us really do.

You are probably not aware that you are writing stories in your mind about everything all the time. Say someone cuts us off on the highway. Our response is "jerk."

The reality may be that the jerk just got the call that his wife is in labor and there are complications, so he's racing to the hospital.

When your wife or husband responds to you with, "What? What do you want?" They may not be angry at you at all. Maybe they just woke up with a splitting headache, and a few moments ago just accidentally kicked the corner of the bed post with their little toe.

Remember that you live in a world full of human beings. We interact with them throughout the day. Each of us has events that occur in our lives all the time. If you work in a company with a thousand employees, it is likely that someone just lost a parent this week. Someone just discovered a small package of drugs in their child's backpack. Someone's spouse was just diagnosed with stage four cancer. Thousands of events can happen to our colleagues or clients in any given week.

Yet when we see someone who is upset, we write a story, we take it personally, rather than just asking what is going on with *them*. We don't ask for clarification; we just assume that we did something wrong, or that the other person is just a jerk. We make it all about us, when we could inquire about them and clear it up.

By the way, that jerk is simultaneously writing a story about how you showed up last week being irritable because your car had a flat tire on the way to work and made you late for an important meeting. But they didn't know any of your story. They just think you are a lazy jerk for showing up late. So now because of their story, they spend all week resenting you.

The truth is that you and the other person are actually good, well-intentioned people who just had a bad day. But we are so busy writing stories and building steam that the other person is a jerk, that the next time we meet, we show up already on edge. This intention is read, and the ball starts rolling. But now both of you, because of your fabricated stories, don't really care for each other anymore. How sad.

The truth really is that 99 percent of the people I have met do not wake up in the morning thinking, "Boy, I can't wait to mess up someone's life today." There is that 1 percent who have so much unresolved emotional baggage, and wrote negative stories for so long, that they have become mean. Out of their pain, they really want to hurt someone today, to take their pain out on someone else.

Here's a summary of our stories:

- They are almost always based on a false reality or a misinterpretation.
- They cause us to react in damaging ways that kill relationships.
- They set the tone for all our interactions with everyone we meet that day.
- They steal our passion and creativity.
- They take the joy out of life.
- Most of the time, reactions are inaccurate, because it's just a story.

If we embrace the fact that we write stories that are not necessarily the truth—and realize that they are just self-created fabrications—we can choose to artificially fabricate positive stories. If someone speaks harshly to me, I can write a story that the person is having a bad day and the response has nothing to do with me. When I do this, I create peace for me, and for them. At this point of staying centered and grounded,

I can now ask that person if they are okay. We can ask if we have done something to cause them harm.

Most of the time the angry person will say something like, "It's not you, I am just having a problem with something right now." And you get to seize the opportunity to say, "I am sorry to hear that. Is there anything I can do to help you?"

Positive stories that I can choose to write will also positively influence my heart in a profound way. If I can artificially write stories that create inspiration, creativity, and passion, then I will automatically act and behave compassionately. When I express compassion, I get different results. It all starts with my thoughts. And thoughts are a choice.

What do you control in your life? Really. What do you *control* in your life? I hear people tell me that they can control their actions. Some say they control their verbal responses to others. In both these instances, have you ever had to apologize to anyone for what you did or said? Of course, you have.

We don't control anything in life except one thing. We can control our thoughts in any given moment. Better stated, you can choose to think any thought you want in any given moment. It's just that we are usually cruising on autopilot and unaware of what we are thinking, and that we have a choice, so we don't seize control of our thoughts. Our thoughts disguise themselves inside our ego. They say, "This is me, it's just what I think."

Why is this behind-the-scenes process of story writing critical to evaluate? Take a look at what is at play:

- **The sum of my thoughts over any given period of time always renders an emotion.** I choose to listen to empowering, positive messages, even if only to mitigate the news.
- **My emotions feed my thoughts and control my actions, words, and behaviors.** I do what I do because I *want* to. It's not enough to need to lose weight, I must want to.

- **My actions, words, and behaviors control my outcomes in life.** What is present in my life is the result of my actions, words, and behaviors. If I want to change my life, I have to change what I do, what I say, and how I behave.

This may seem like a lot of up-front work to be mindful about, to pay attention to what thoughts you think. But as you do this, you will notice that your emotions change, so you get a reward, which makes it more compelling to continue. After a little while this process starts to alter your personality to be generally more positive. At this point you will notice that positive thoughts seem to occur more naturally. This is what I call the momentum of thought. You can change your habit of thought.

You and I write stories about everything. And we will never stop. But we can notice that we are writing stories and see them for what they are: simple fabrications. By seeing them for what they are, we can set them aside and become free of their power. We can ask the other person what's going on, and ask if we said or did something to warrant what they believe is hurtful. We can stop and evaluate the circumstances, become unbiased, to see the black-and-white truth better. This freedom from stories will empower you to create from scratch anything you want. What I am describing is a self-directed life, not one flying on autopilot.

TAKEAWAYS

- Blame causes disconnection with people. And our life's goals are dependent on relationships.

- If I get hurt by what someone says, there might be a speck of truth in what they are saying. If there were no truth in their statement, we would just laugh it off.
- Reexamine the painful past. See if you can rewrite the story to remove all negative emotions about what happened.
- If you find you were at some fault, then go back to that person and clean it up. When we do this, guilt and shame disappear.
- Without emotional baggage of the past, we are free and can't be knocked off our center again.
- Be careful. Our made-up stories can generate more fear inside us and create fear in others. This is not profitable as a leader.
- We write stories in our head to fill in the gaps that black-and-white data leave unfilled. We do this because we want certainty. Our ego thinks that certainty of failure, even based on a made-up story, is better than the unknown. Your ego thinks it is better to prepare for the worst.
- Negative stories take on a life of their own and damage possibility.
- The stories we write in our heads are almost never a true reflection of the real truth.
- We can seize the power of any situation when we, on purpose, write positive stories about what is going to happen. Positive or negative, they are both still made up, but the positive one will help you find answers while you build connection with others.

9

WHERE ARE THE WOMEN? POWERHOUSES OF LEADERSHIP

By now you are probably asking, "Where are the women in your examples of leadership?" That's a fair question. And I hate my answer.

It is so sad for me to have to admit that of the 4,500 executives I have enjoyed working with, I have only gotten the chance to work with maybe thirty women. Maybe it's the high-tech industry I chose. Maybe it's the societal flaw that is being experienced by me in the world not letting women rise to the position of VP or CEO. I don't know. But in general it bothers me a great deal.

I am impressed by the women I have enjoyed coaching. I am happy to say that at the time of this writing, I am working with two incredible women. They are important to their organizations and highly respected.

Up front let me say, as leaders, women are naturally better than men in many ways. Here's what I have experienced working with them, but I won't attempt to explain why I think these valuable personal virtues are present. Women just seem to excel in these areas:

- Women exhibit more caring and empathy for their teams than men do, which creates much better understanding and connection within their teams.
- They seem to be more clear-headed. They see the underlying truth of any situation much better than men. I think men

can get caught up in rationalizations and denials because of how they perceive a man should act. Women don't have those filters to have to clear away to be able to see the truth in the raw facts.

- Women can be more direct. They seem to be better communicators. They don't hesitate to speak the truth. They cut to the chase.
- They often embrace the idea of commitment faster than men. They don't seem to have as much fear of commitment as men do. They are more willing to be bold and on mission. It may be that men are afraid of falling off the white stallion, and so they hesitate.
- Women are often better able to see the big picture. They can see the interpersonal consequences of a decision, while men seem to be more blind to the impact on individuals and the dynamics that could be rendered onto a team.
- The women I have had the blessing to coach seem to care more. Success, struggles, and trials are more personal to them. They are more personally engaged. They don't discount or rationalize away problems as easily as men do, and that's sad for men in leadership.

Victoria was the CEO of a high-tech start-up several years ago. She had recently left a major corporation as a VP of a division to take this new role. She was an outstanding success at her previous company and launched a major piece of new business that basically saved the company. If I told you the name of the company she left, every one of you reading this would readily recognize the name.

During our first meeting I could sense that she was tense. Like with every client, I told her that I was making a complete commitment to her success and did not, and would not, judge her for anything she was to say.

We stumbled for a few moments trying to find that interpersonal connection between each other. There was clearly something in the way, between us, which was strange for me. Finally, she said that she was uncomfortable about how it felt to seek a man's help for her to be successful. Her experience was that if she became vulnerable and sought the help of a man in business, she would be judged as not good enough.

I told her that thousands of men had sought my help. I went on to explain that many of the men I had coached had actually teared up or cried as we worked together.

At that moment both of us saw the problem. We both understood the discomfort and distance that existed between men and women in the business environment. It wasn't a problem between Victoria and me; it was a problem in our culture between men and women.

I challenged both of us to become bold and take risks and take all the considerations of gender we were noticing and throw them out the window. I told her that it would take some work on both our parts to constantly see each other as gender neutral. And yet, we did just that.

Victoria opened up and told me that the first issue she had was how to work with men who reported to her. She told me that she knew what to do and would give guidance to her direct reports about what she saw they could accomplish, and she would offer help to these men about how to grow in their careers. She said she was uncomfortable, however, doing that because of how the man might react to receiving the help of a woman in his career.

If a man who reported up to her needed to be corrected, reprimanded, supported, or guided, she was afraid that she would come off as a bitch. Where a man could say exactly the same things and the direction would be accepted. She continued, "But if I avoid the bitch scenario and am kind and supportive, then I am afraid that I would look soft, loving, tender, kind, with no backbone." I could see in her eyes that she felt she was in a no-win situation.

A big part of her problem, I told her, was that she was holding her gender as a consideration. That her attachment as to how she showed up to the team of men was causing her to try to modify her actions, behavior, and speech to gain their acceptance and respect. And that this attempt would never work.

I challenged her to be herself, to be authentically who she is. Forget how the men were going to receive her leadership. It is their responsibility to hold respect for the office she holds.

I said, "If you take your personal consideration off the table, then you improve the chances that men would take it off the table too."

I told her that she makes a perfect Victoria, but a lousy fabrication of who she thought she should be. I counseled, "If you don't hold it in your heart that men will not connect with you, then they might not hold it as an obstacle also. You have a job to do. Just do it. And do it your way. Get your thinking off yourself. You don't have to prove yourself to anyone. You hold the job title and are competent to be great at it. Be great at it. Think about helping the men on your team to grow. Focus on the business success and say everything you have to say, regardless of their reaction."

She was listening. Then I said, "I want you to become oblivious to their reaction to you, not hypersensitive to it. As a woman CEO, you are a pioneer. It's tough pioneering, but just like for the men, I am here for you to win massive success. I am not coaching a woman or a man. I am coaching a CEO who happens to be human."

Victoria did an outstanding job. Just like so many other companies I have worked with, the product wasn't a spectacular fit for the market. But she did do a merger/acquisition and went on to be in a C-suite role for another major high-tech firm today. I am sure she has much more wealth than I do, and she has earned every penny of it.

Look, we need to accept that people have considerations about gender today. My responsibility is to take those considerations and throw them away. Maybe we will see the day that we as the human race can become blind to gender, race, and sexual preference. Maybe when we are blind to differences, we can fully embrace each other, love one another, support one another as equals, and become solid teams.

TAKEAWAYS

- All of us need to drop any consideration about men versus women in a leadership role.
- It's our internal stories that lead to subconscious beliefs about gender. These stories often keep the gender gap going.
- Someday we may all wake up and become blind to gender or race. And that would be a welcome day for our society and business.

10

DARE TO DREAM—FIND YOUR COURAGE

One of the most courageous acts you can do in life is to face your past emotional pains and the poor self-image they have caused—and still dare to dream of a brilliant future for yourself and your family. Easier said than done. Let me prove it to you. What are your dreams for the future? I don't mean intellectual goals. I mean dreams that give you goose bumps.

I am writing about allowing your subconscious mind to render visions of hope, success, and adventure that moves your heart. A dream is something that you can mentally visualize with detail, something you could describe with all the glory that the grand vision would bring. The difference between a goal and a dream is this: While a goal may be specific, interesting, and worthwhile, a dream will stir your heart with positive emotion.

It's time we tap into the incredible power of the subconscious mind and use it through visualization to dream of a beautiful future. When we do this, we tap into the power of our emotions to drive us toward our dreams. This is where the real power in your life will be found.

My client Henry was the CEO of a new high-tech start-up. I told him that I would help him succeed through coaching, but to do so, I would need to know exactly what he wanted so I could be clear in helping him get there.

I said, "Give me my MBO [manage by objective] to accomplish. What do you want, and give me as much detail of what success would look like for you, so I can taste it too?"

Of course, he hadn't thought about his success in this way, so he had no answer. I encouraged him to dig a little deeper with these prompts:

- I am paid as your coach by the corporation, so I am committed to returning an ROI on my fee to the corporation. What does the corporation want? It wants me to assist you in maximizing stakeholder value. This is a monetary objective.
- So from a monetary point of view, realizing that you, as the CEO, are also a stakeholder, how much money would you like to create for yourself out of this play, and by what date?
- When you give me a dollar amount that you would like to personally make, and knowing that you own 3 percent of the outstanding stock options, we can create however much money the whole company would have to be worth to extrapolate your 3 percent and have it match the dollar amount of your personal goal.
- But much more importantly, why do you want this amount of money? What would you do with it? Pretend that you had that money in your hand today, what would you do?

I worked through this line of questioning, and when I got to the part about what he'd do with the money, he paused for about four seconds and finally said, "Oh, I don't know. I am pretty well set. Maybe I'd do something for my sister."

I pressed him to tell me more.

"Well Mom and Dad weren't really there when we were growing up, so my sister basically raised me. Even though she is only a couple of years older, I think of her more as my mom than my real mother. Really, I don't know how I would have survived without her."

I told Henry to keep going.

As he did, I saw how much love and compassion he felt for his sister. He even needed to pause because his emotions were so strong. "She has a hard life. She married a real loser. She had two boys with him, and then he left her. She now lives in Colorado with her boys and works two jobs as a waitress. I go and see her as often as I can, and when I pull up in front of her house, she always runs out to meet me."

I asked, "What do you think you would do for her if you achieved your goal of massive success?"

He paused for a few seconds. Then with new excitement he said, "I would pay off her house."

I invited him to visualize what paying off her house might look like. I asked him to mentally play out the movie of handing her the deed and seeing her reaction. He did. Henry teared, looked away, and had nothing more to say.

I knew I had accomplished my goal—which was to help him find his powerful and passionate reason to succeed.

Three years later, after Henry and his team did their IPO, and he achieved significant wealth, I asked him how the dream of helping his sister unfolded. With great satisfaction he told me the story.

"I contacted her mortgage company and paid off her house. I called her up and told her that I wanted to drop by to see her. With the grant deed in my pocket, I drove up and parked in front of her house. Like many times before, she saw me drive up and came scurrying out of the house to meet me in the front yard. We hugged each other like we always did and exchanged greetings.

"Then I pulled out the grant deed to her house and handed it to her. She asked what the envelope was for, and then she opened it and just stared at the paper. She didn't comprehend what it meant.

"I told her that what she had up until today was a trust deed, which says you have legal right to the house, but the bank really owned it. This is a grant deed, which says that you completely own the house. There is no more mortgage payment."

I explained to her that I had been richly blessed in business and wanted to do this for her. I told her how much she meant to me, and that I wouldn't be where I was without her love and support. I told her that I also set up a trust account that would pay her $5,000 a month for the rest of her life. I encouraged her to go back to school and get the degree and career she had always wanted.

"It took a minute for this to sink in. She wanted to refuse, but she knew she couldn't. It dawned on her that she could quit both jobs, return to school, and be home every night for the boys. As it all sank in, she just lost it and began to cry."

He said, "She grabbed me and hugged me tight. Then her knees buckled, and she sank to the lawn and sobbed tears of joy. Dan, the experience on the lawn was overwhelming for both her and me. It was greater than I could have ever imagined. My heart was bursting with joy, and still is today, when I think about it."

For me, as an executive coach, *that* was one of my best days. I teared up at Henry's story. I saw the pure joy and contentment in his eyes. That was just one of the few days when it was reaffirmed that I wouldn't trade this career for anything in the world.

I talk about the money involved with success, because I owe the corporation an ROI on their investment in me. But for the client, it is usually never about the material gain, as in greed. It is about what the money can do for the people they love. Almost every time I am with a CEO in a conversation about money, it is rarely what they would buy for themselves. It is almost always about how they would use the money for someone they love.

FIND THE COURAGE TO DREAM

What is a dream? I believe dreams are a collection of images that create a story usually replete with emotions. Of course they appear in our minds during sleep. The meanings behind our dreams and why we have them is often obscure to us.

Have you ever had a nightmare and when you awake you feel fearful? Do you notice that a gripping nightmare can have an impact on your entire day? People say, "I had this dream last night, and I just can't seem to shake it." Dreams can be powerful. Remember, they are images, ideas, emotions, and sensations, but the most important point to remember about dreams is that they are visions you experience emotionally.

How about dreaming during the waking hours of the day. Can we daydream? Of course we can, and you have done it thousands of times. Daydreams allow us to get lost in a story for a few moments. Daydreams include vivid images, ideas, emotions, and sensations. Daydreams take the conscious mind out of the loop and let the subconscious mind kind of go where it wants.

The important point here is that dreams alter your emotions in a deeply profound way. When you dream, you know you have tapped into a power much greater than the conscious mind could ever deliver. Your great question might be, "Can I harness the power of daydreams to alter my state of being to be more powerful? Can I alter the context in how I view the world and find power to achieve what I dare dream is possible?" The answer is yes.

You can use the conscious mind to create and send a query, on purpose, to the subconscious mind to tap into this power. I call this power daydreaming. Power daydreaming occurs when you find a thought that sparks a flame of passion. Some idea that moves your heart to want it to come true. Then you carefully nurture that idea, shutting off the Debbie Downer ego of play-it-safe thoughts. Come back at least three times a day and take moments to ponder the idea that gave you inspiration. Feed the dream with contemplation. The passion to have the dream come true will grow. And at some point, your wish turns into commitment.

We tap into the subconscious mind by asking it a question like, "What would I really want, if I could have anything?" When we ask this question, we have to believe the subconscious mind will render an answer.

Then we quiet our busy mind and stay with the question. Sometimes the answer appears right away, but more often than not the subconscious mind will render the answer a few hours or a few days later. The answer usually comes as an epiphany. The epiphany has deep feeling with it, so you can be confident that it's your answer.

These insights usually come when you are in the craziest of places: on the toilet, in the shower, or driving on the highway. They occur when your conscious mind puts down the microphone and you don't have to think about what you are doing, but you are also occupied and can't do anything else at the moment. It is in these moments that the subconscious can speak.

The subconscious mind is meek and polite. It will not shove the conscious mind out of the way and grab the microphone to tell you something. It waits until the conscious mind is finished talking, which is rare and short-lived.

A dream pulls us forward. Most of us live on autopilot just sort of waiting to see how things turn out. But that leaves too much to random chance because waiting to see how things turn out robs you of control. Don't depend on fate, destiny, luck, or random good fortune to fix everything wrong with your life. Do more.

You would think that dreaming about a brilliant future would be fun. But as we get a little life under our belt, we discover that often it is not. If you don't believe me, just ask anyone what their dreams are. Daring to dream brings up three powerful roadblocks:

- Dreaming makes us face our self-image. When we dare to dream of something great and wonderful, like something we have never experienced before, our brain will tell us that it's not reasonable. Your conscious mind will want to shut down the dream. It will say: "Just look at your past. Who do you think you are to dare to dream of such a beautiful thing you've never done or had before? You have no evidence in your past that indicates you deserve better."

- Over time, our ego has developed a standard of who it says we are and what is possible for us. Dreaming wants to expand that border of what is possible, but it often flies in the face of our self-image. Remember, ego created your self-image, and it needs to be right. It loves to stand on the ground of certainty. And it doesn't like change.
- Dreaming triggers fear. What if we dream and go for our goals but they don't come to pass? At any age over thirty you have learned a lot about life. You have more wisdom to see all the obstacles that stand in the way of your dream, should you even dare to have one. These "facts" bring up fear, which in turn keeps us small and avoids the pain of disappointment. The ego would be just fine, in fact, quite happy, if you stayed small and safe. In fact, the ego would be very happy if nothing in your life ever changed.

You have two powerful forces working against you when it comes to dreaming of a brighter future. Which means that in order to dream, you need courage. Think of courage as starting fluid. When you work on a small engine that hasn't been started for a while, you take a can of starting fluid and spray some into the throat of the carburetor. Starting fluid is incredibly combustible. If there is a spark in the cylinder, the engine will pop and try to ignite. This initial pop often gets gas from the carburetor flowing into the cylinder.

Sometimes, all it takes to get the engine running is a small initial start. Courage is the starting fluid you need to power daydream. Courage can be seen when you take the first step toward your dream. And when you take your first step because you had courage to dream, you find moments of inspiration. Keep the inspiration going.

IF NOTHING CHANGES, NOTHING CHANGES

One principle that is critical to success is letting go of the past. This is hard, but incredibly important. You are you. You are not your past. But when we fail to embrace this truth, we show up today the same way we did yesterday and, no surprise, get the same results. When we operate on autopilot, we repeat the past, which reinforces our internal story that the autopilot life is the truth for you. This autopilot state also tricks our mind to believe that the past does indeed control our future. This is all going on subconsciously, of course, which makes this dynamic a most insidious and powerful inhibitor to our future.

Who you are today is actually a limitless possibility. Because this new day has not been spent or written, it is all raw possibility. Today is a blank canvas, full of possibility. The past brought you here, but it doesn't have to define who you will become today or tomorrow. We tend to look at our lives through the lens of our past. This approach to life dictates that our future can be no better than our past. This is insane. This moment, this day, has never been seen or experienced before. This day is not a hand-me-down from yesterday. It can be whatever you choose it to be. But all too often we throw the opportunity away because we ignorantly look at our future through the lens of the past.

Next time you get in your car, notice the size of the windshield as compared to the size of the rearview mirror. Detroit builds automobiles in a certain way. Where do you think the automobile designers want you to spend your visual time when driving down the highway of life? That's right, 95 percent of your visual time should be looking out the windshield, and only 5 percent glancing in the rearview mirror. Any avoidable accident will appear in front of you. Keep staring into the rearview mirror and bam. Another wreck.

If nothing changes, nothing changes. We have to initiate something new and different to ignite change. When it comes to dreaming of a brighter future, this change starts with a decision, followed by an action.

This new action can be and will be possible only because of a new passion. Your passion will be sparked from a dream or a vision that excites you. This is only possible when we stare out the windshield toward the future 95 percent of the time, and spend only 5 percent glancing back at the past.

The hardest part of coaching is helping my clients discover what they really want. Once they find their dream, the rest of the work is much easier. Finding the dream, their why, is difficult because most clients resist dreaming of a brighter future. When I see a restlessness present when we talk about positive dreams for their life, I know it's about subtle fear. Fear of falling in love with an idea, only to be disappointed.

Let's try it. What do you want? Suspend all analytical or intellectual filters. Get in touch with the deepest part of your being. What would you love to have, do, be, or accomplish? We can't move forward until you discover that deep and hidden dream within you.

Here is the exercise I have used thousands of times. While it works much better face-to-face, please be open and willing and take this exercise by pretending that I am in front of you right now.

It's critical for me to know what you want in life. As a coach, I can't help you get what you want unless you know yourself, and then tell me. I want to help you discover your true desires.

If I had a magic wand and waved it over you right now, and you could have, be, or do anything, what would you love? No kidding. You can't fail in this moment. Anything is possible. Go there in your heart. Dig. What do you truly want in your heart? Ignore your conscious ego chatter right now. Get quiet and capture your heart's desire. While we're at it, clear all the shallow wants like a new car or a bigger house. Go for the holy grail. What do you deeply want?

What would give you goose bumps if you could have it. At this point in time, I am looking for you to begin to fidget and maybe tear up a little. Now I say, "That's it. What just came up for you that you want to discount as not really possible?"

This is critical work right here and now. Don't move on until you capture your heart's deepest desire. Clear the decks of all thoughts and wander through your mind, staying in the question. What would be great? What do you really want? What is your deepest calling? What would give you goose bumps if you dared to dream of getting it?

When you find the glimpse of the dream that moves you, stop and write down one paragraph about what it is. Right now. Take thirty seconds and capture it. Keep that paragraph handy. We are going to need that later.

I promise you that you can have what you just wrote down. I know you think I am crazy, but you really can. If someone told me that Elon Musk could create a private company that would take over from NASA in delivering supplies to the space station, and then bring the booster rockets back and land them safely on a floating barge, I would have told them they were crazy. But he did it.

I really need you to have a little faith, a glimpse of hope that you can have what you just wrote down. If you feel you can't, then have a little faith in me because I know you can have the life of your dreams.

HAPPINESS IS AN INSIDE JOB

If nothing changes, nothing changes. If you were to continue doing what you are doing, and getting the same results, is that okay with you? Really? If you feel as if there must be something more than what you are getting out of life, then we can begin to see the need for change. Remember, insanity is wanting something more and different, yet resisting the change to make it happen.

Happiness is an inside job. It all starts with you.

I want these words to leverage a deep desire in you to find the courage to change. I want you to begin hating autopilot or status quo in your life. I know where you are. You are reading this book. You must want something different than what you have.

Take a moment and dare to dream that you are, in fact, worthy.

Dream that you deserve a better future than you have today. Dare to dream that it is not only possible but in your grasp to achieve. What do you really want? Dig deep here. What is hidden inside you and buried under self-image, and obstacles, and all the considerations you can come up with? What if anything were possible? What if you had the time, money, and support in great supply to have your dream come true? What would you love to happen? Believe for a moment. Believe in yourself. Believe in your future. What would you want?

Do you want to buy a house and car for every member of your family? Do you want to send your sister to college? Do you want to return to college yourself? Do you want to shoot for the moon?

Your subconscious mind is gullible. It will begin to believe whatever you tell it. It doesn't matter if you *feel* it's the truth; the point is that your subconscious mind is listening when you speak about the future. Good or bad. So be very careful. When you are speaking or writing stories in your head about yourself and your future, the most important person is listening—you. It matters that you choose to speak into your life what you want instead of what you don't want, or keep repeating the stories about what stands in the way.

What do you want in your life? What would be so cool that you would feel excited? Once you come upon an inspirational idea, start to visualize the accomplishment of that dream as if it were already present in your life today. I want you to be so clear about what your dream looks like that you can quickly describe it in full, colorful detail.

It was about 1986 when I went to a seminar. During the seminar we did an exercise. We were paired in twos. I sat across from a young woman in her twenties. We were sitting face-to-face with our knees almost touching.

Here was the exercise. I was to ask her this one question: What do you want? Then I was to repeat the question when she stopped speaking. I was to only ask the same question over and over. The exercise was designed to empty out her brain of all the things she thought she wanted and to dig into her heart to discover what she really wanted. This exercise was to go on like this for ten minutes.

I asked, "What do you want?" She continued to answer with items and concepts such as a new car, pay off her bills, a promotion, go to a rock concert, new clothes, losing ten pounds. She went on and on, and every time she stopped talking, I asked again, "What do you want?"

Finally she was intellectually empty. She didn't have anything else to say. I kept asking. Then she put her head down and started to sob. I was instructed not to touch her. She just sat there and cried. At the end of the exercise I asked her what came up for her. Her answer made me cry. She looked up with tear-filled eyes and said, "I just want my dad to love me."

We have to get out of our head and dig into our hearts to find what really moves us. This is where your passion lies.

Stop reading now and pry into your subconscious mind and dare to dream. Find the nugget that gives you goose bumps. Picture what you would feel like and what others would say to you once you have your dream. Tell me a story about your dream. Then write it down. Please dare to dream.

TAKEAWAYS

- It takes courage to dream of a brighter future that is better than you have ever experienced.
- Ask yourself questions about what you truly want in life. Your questions settle into the subconscious mind as a query. The subconscious already knows what you really want, and it will render the answer as a spark of a new passion.

- Just like Henry, your dreams will build passion which will become your mission, which will drive your behaviors, which will render the accomplishment of your dream.
- Take time during your day to ask the big question, and let your mind wander on purpose toward the answer to your question. The subconscious will render an answer when you silence your conscious mind.
- You will know when you have found the seed of a new passion when you feel excited or emotionally moved by its vision.
- Your ego will want to kill the passion of your dream the moment after you feel it.
- You realize the need for a dream when you discover you don't really have one that moves you.
- Let the seedling of your new dream take hold. Don't let the ego pull it up. When it becomes a sapling, then it can survive the ego who wants to kill it.
- The subconscious mind is gullible. It will believe any story your conscious mind tells it.

11

PASSION IGNITES COMMITMENT

About sixteen years ago I worked with a CEO, David, and many of his team members. Back then his team had created new and disruptive technology and was in the midst of finding their strategic vision. One weekend I facilitated an offsite executive team workshop focusing on how heightened passion drives commitment, and authentic commitment drives achievement.

The team spent hours discussing next steps. I asked them a direct and specific question: "Of all the ideas on the table, which one will offer the best promise of fantastic success? To clarify my question, which one could offer 30 percent top-line quarter over quarter revenue growth?"

This narrowed the conversation down quickly, and they landed on telecom. We spent the next day establishing strategic milestones for the telecom space with dates of accomplishment, which, if achieved, would put them on a path for massive success. The summary of the offsite was distilled down to five major strategic goals for their product in the telecom space.

At the time, everyone felt these were wonderful aspirations but were going to be really difficult, requiring a great deal of work as well as a lot of luck. They were passionate about the goals, but I asked for their commitment to the strategic goals. In the wellspring of passion, even in the face of a lack of evidence as to how they would get them done, they committed.

I asked them to affirm their commitment to the goals by standing up. I wanted commitment to be voluntary and public. The CEO jotted down the five goals and slid the paper into his pocket.

Two years later, after the company penetrated the telecom space and was growing virally, they did an IPO, and it was brilliant. A couple of years after the IPO, David pulled out that original piece of paper where the five goals were written and held them up for the team to see. They were surprised that they had accomplished all five in the time frame they had committed to. When we wrote them, the team admitted they were aspirational ideals, but there was a lot of doubt about their veracity. But since they truly felt passionate about the goals, they committed.

A NEW LINCOLN FOR THE MAIL CARRIER

A passionate vision is a motion picture, or a video. Motion pictures are full of visual and audio detail. That is why they are so engaging. Even a power daydream can be watched by the mind's eye, and they can be described in colorful, concrete language and with specific detail.

Once you have a nugget of a dream that excites you, it is critical to build detail into your vision of what success looks like and to see the vision or dream as if it were already accomplished, as well as to envision what feelings you would experience once your dream is accomplished.

You want to picture yourself in the dream and live it out in your mind. At the moment of success, what will your spouse or partner say about your accomplishment? Picture their face and tell me what they would say to you as they raise a glass to toast you. What would your mom and dad say when they learn of your success? With success in hand, what would you now be able to do for someone close to you? How would you celebrate on the day you have a milestone of success? Who would you take to dinner to celebrate? What restaurant would you go to? What table there do you want reserved? What gift would you pull out from under the table and give to your significant other and then say, "Thank you for supporting me in going after this dream." What would they say back to you? In your mind's eye, can you see their face as they respond to your gift?

A dream must have clarity and specificity to be powerful. Stop reading, find your dream that gives you goose bumps, as we discussed in the last chapter, and picture it now. Not just the dream but work to artificially experience the glory of that dream accomplished, live the moment of success in your mind as a vision, and savor what it feels like to have a goal or a dream in the bag.

One client of mine did not need much encouragement to express his dream of success.

Al told me, "I grew up in New Jersey where my dad was a postal worker. He is a really good man, good father, and we love each other dearly. Every few years Dad would buy a new car. His dream car was the Lincoln Mark series, like the Mark III or Mark IV. But on his salary, he could never afford such luxury. Dad had to compromise and buy a Mercury Marquis. He would always tell his friends: 'The Mercury Marquis is built on the same chassis as the Lincoln Mark series.' He would compare how much they were alike."

My client told me how it saddened him to hear his dad make these comparisons because it was clear that he really wanted a Lincoln Mark. Al told me, "I am determined that when I finally get the big M/A or IPO, I will buy Dad a new Lincoln Mark series car."

I asked Al to take a few moments and describe the day he was to present his dad with a new Lincoln, minute by minute. Al did his best to create how it would go. The more he described his dream, the more excited he became.

A couple of years later, after the liquidity event for his company was complete, and he had earned the big pile of cash, I saw Al again. I asked him to tell me the story about the actual event of giving his dad the Lincoln. His face lit up as he described the realization of his dream.

"I flew to my hometown and took a cab to the local Lincoln dealership. I walked in, looked at the different Mark models they had on the lot, and found one in Dad's favorite color. It was spectacular, equipped with all the options money could buy. I wrote a check for the full price. Next, I bought a one-foot-wide red ribbon with a three-foot bow. When I pulled up to the house, I parked in the driveway, but just out of sight of the living room window. I walked next door to my dad's neighbor, who I had known for decades, and told him what I was about to do. I asked him to wait five minutes, then come over and knock on the door, and when Dad answers, tell him he has to come outside to move his car. Don't wait for Dad to reason with you, just make your statement and walk away.

"I walked up to Dad's door. He saw me coming, opened the door, and gave me a big tearful hug. After the five minutes had elapsed, there was a knock on the door, right on time. The neighbor told Dad to move his car and then walked away. Frustrated at the interruption of our reunion, Dad apologized to me and set out for the driveway. When he rounded the corner, there it was. Big, new, beautiful, topped with that big red bow.

"Dad stood there in silence. He just stared at it. He didn't turn and look at me for at least ten seconds. I finally walked up to him from behind and put my hand on his shoulder. He looked back over to me with glassy eyes full of disbelief. He didn't say a word. So I did.

"'Dad, I have been richly blessed recently. I credit much of my success to how you brought me up and what you taught me in life. I know how much you appreciate the Lincoln automobile. It is my pleasure to give back a little something for how much you mean to me.'

"Now tears were streaming down Dad's face, and he began to shake as he tried not to openly cry on the driveway. After all, his neighbor was only twenty feet away, smiling as broadly as me."

Here is a side note, which may greatly help you with your dream of what you really want. Almost 90 percent of the time with over 4,500 clients, when I ask a client what would give them goose bumps if they could have or do something powerful with success, they tell me about how they want to give or do for someone close to them. The response I get to the question of a dream is rarely about what the client would buy for themselves.

What would you do or give to someone you love?

You deserve to have your own "Lincoln in the driveway story." If anything were possible, what would you do? What would you give to someone, that you know would change their life?

COMMITMENT VS TRYING

Think of all the people you have worked with. When you asked them to start a project, or complete a task, what did they say?

"Well, hopefully, if Bill finishes his work on time, we should get it done."

"You can count on me and my team to do everything possible to make that happen."

"We are going to really try."

"We will do our very best to accomplish what you ask."

In these instances of *hopefully, do everything possible, really try*, or *do our very best*, how many times as a percentage over your entire career did those teams accomplish what you asked them to do—right and on time?

The average answer I get is 30 percent.

Now think of the rare team members who respond with, "You have my word and my commitment. We will do it."

Of these rare people who offer heartfelt, authentic commitment, how many times, as a percentage, did they get it done right and on time? The average response I get is 95 percent.

Wait a minute. Are you telling me from your experience there is a 65 percent increased chance of success when someone's actions come from heartfelt commitment? When we operate from the context of commitment, success is almost assured. What were your statistical answers to these two questions? Did you discover in your experience that there was 65 percent increased success rate with commitment over *do my best*? Would you like a 65 percent increased chance for success? Of course you would.

If there is a significant increased chance of success when we come from commitment, why don't we all just commit? We know commitment leverages increased success. Here's the reason. If we come from *hopefully, really try,* or *do my best*, we keep a back door of escape for failure. If we don't succeed, there is no blame. "We really did try to make it." We are already anticipating failure. "Hey I told you I would do my best, and we did our best. What do you want from me better than my best?"

It may seem unreasonable to ask someone for a commitment when facing an unknown future. "Hey, I won't commit because I can't see all the things I am going to run into, which could make this task impossible. All I can do is really try." But success in the world is unreasonable. It is never reasonable to say that you will enjoy massive success. And in the future, unknown obstacles will stand in our way. So with this scenario, we can never commit.

When you find a vision that ignites a passion, and you revisit that vision at least three times a day for a month, you will find that your passion will grow. Your passion will grow to a point of your wanting to make a commitment. When you commit, you notice that most of your fears and considerations that stand in the way just disappear. At this moment of commitment fueled by passion, you are on a mission with purpose. You have left the world of autopilot and the excuse of *let's see how it turns out* behind. In this space, your chances of success are at least 95 percent.

Try is safe because you can't be blamed. But we fail to see that just trying makes us play a very small game in life. But we remember that the ego's main job is to keep you away from pain. It wants you to listen to fear, even if it costs you a brilliant future. There is no brilliant life in just seeing how it will turn out. Lacking that passion and commitment, we wonder why we are emotionally empty. Like a hamster on a wheel, we exert lots of energy, but usually go nowhere. There is no grand mission. No risk for failure. Nothing is at stake. It is a small game.

I am always looking for the common denominator of success. I look for the key element that is always present in massively successful teams. And I have found that everything filters down from the top, so I also want to identify the key elements in a great leader. And I found them.

I have coached four executives personally who have worked directly for Bill Gates, Steve Jobs, Larry Ellison, and Michael Dell.

During my coaching of these four direct reports to the captains of industry, I got the chance to talk to them about Bill, Steve, Larry, and Michael. They were generous with their information and this is what I discovered: two common denominators. The first one disturbed me at first. All four dropped out of college. It can't be that a lack of formal education was instrumental to success. But what I found was that these leaders' passion for creating success was so extreme that they simply had to leave school to get started on their mission. I also found that the lack of formal training could have helped unlock possibilities that they wouldn't have considered if they were operating with a formally constrained mind.

The second common denominator was what I suspected might be the real answer to their success. I asked my clients who worked for these champions of business about their bosses' passion. I asked, "Rate him on a scale of 1 to 10 and tell me how large his passion was for creating massive success."

Their answers were all exactly the same, and that surprised me. Each direct report responded exactly the same and without hesitation by rating their boss's passion as 11 or 12.

I reminded them that I gave them a range of 1 to 10. They each stuck with their answer. "Hey, he was off the scale with passion." "He bent the needle on the passion gauge." "He was a maniac on a mission." "He was a zealot for success."

I have found, without exception, that super-heightened levels of personal passion are the common denominator to success. Now don't misunderstand me, passion does not always look like exuberance, or is necessarily loud. Passion can look like quiet resolve. But super-heightened levels of passion always result in commitment. And it is commitment that renders results. These four—Bill Gates, Steve Jobs, Larry Ellison, and Michael Dell—just couldn't be messed with when trouble or obstacles came to visit. They stayed the course.

To summarize, follow this critical line of thinking:

- Find a goal that gives you goose bumps and ignites your passion.
- Nurture your passion so it gets strong enough for you to want to commit.
- Know that commitment almost always ensures massive success.
- Getting things done is execution traction.
- Predictable execution traction increases your company stock price.

Use these five points to inspire your team and move them to become unstoppable. When they feel the passion and decipher the map to success, they will most certainly follow you on the journey, even into battle. When you clearly believe, they will too.

BLACK DOG/WHITE DOG

There are many versions of something called the black dog/white dog story. It goes something like this:

> *A Native American elder once described his own inner struggles in this manner: "Inside of me there are two dogs. One of the dogs is mean and evil. The other dog is good. The mean dog fights the good dog all the time." When asked which dog wins, he reflected for a moment and replied, "The one I feed the most."*

Which dog are you feeding? The black dog that listens to all your fears and has you playing safe, or the white dog that encourages you to love your people, to inspire them, to lead them courageously into the market battle, giving all the credit away to your team? To be remembered as a loving, courageous, passionate CEO?

Get clear about this one thing. All of this is a choice. It's your choice how you want your life to turn out. You don't have to live on autopilot. Once you recognize that you have a choice, then you have a responsibility to make a decision. Don't just turn the page to the next chapter. I call you out to decide. Right here and now. Because, like I stated earlier, I am committed to your success regardless of whether or not you decide to cave in on your future. So stop for a minute now—and choose.

You see, I truly do believe in you.

TAKEAWAYS

- Your vision is like a movie you have created in your mind. It has detail and a story.
- When nurtured, passion turns into commitment. And you get what you are committed to, not necessarily what you wish for or want.
- Commitment empowers you to take consistent, bold action toward your dream.
- Super-heightened levels of passion are always present in massive success.
- You nurture your passion by becoming aware of the thoughts you think. If they are positive, you build passion. If they are negative, you fuel your fear.

12

"PRIDE GOETH BEFORE A FALL"

This chapter would be easy if I just told the stories of a few CEOs who achieved massive success and then stumbled and fell because of their pride. I could easily point out the few clients who changed after success, how money did change them, but in negative ways. I could talk about how they drank their own Kool-Aid and became more self-centered, selfish, and self-seeking. I could tell you that their prideful arrogance made them unrelatable to all those who were friends. I could tell you a couple of stories about their pride, and ego, which led to affairs, broken marriages, and ultimately financial failure of their plays. Fortunately, these are few in my experience, very few.

If I were to give more attention to the negative, that would not lead you to the light. I want to give you bullet points to look out for in your own life, so you can avoid their pitfalls. That seems profitable to you, the reader, without playing too long in what not to do. I have found that it is much more beneficial to study what to do, than what not to do. If you golf, how does it work out for you to concentrate on not slicing the ball? When you focus on the negative, you accidentally source that into existence. Here is my short list of three big traits to avoid:

- **Selfish, self-centered, and self-seeking.** Your title does not allow you to become selfish in your thinking. A leadership position is not a position of privilege. We no longer have parking spots in the company lot with the name of the CEO on it. We don't have executive washrooms. We don't do two martini lunches on Friday with other CEOs. You need to focus all your attention on the team. You are there to support them, not glorify or satisfy yourself. Constantly check in on your emotions. Look to see what you are feeling. If you are restless, irritable, or discontented, then you are thinking about yourself. Think about that last sentence for a moment. You are in a leadership position to support, encourage, guide, direct, build, and replace members to create a team. When you think of yourself, that is the fastest way to have the team alienate themselves from you.

- **Pride.** The birthplace of blind spots. When you notice your heart swell with pride, kill it, even though it feels great. When you begin to think that you are all that, and a bag of chips, look out. You are missing something that is about to bite you. Pride will encourage you to make poor decisions based on what you think you deserve, not on what the market or the team needs. When you get prideful, so will the team, and that's when you will find divisions in the ranks. They will start to argue and fight.

- **Unchecked fear.** A little fear is natural. It reminds you to check on things. It keeps you careful. But when fear gets out of hand, look out. You will start hesitating too long. You will start making decisions that lead to safety, not glory. When you are pioneering in new breakthrough areas of market, technology, or really anywhere, you need to be bold. There is never any evidence when you are pioneering to prove to yourself that you are on the right track. Fear, like passion, is contagious. When you sneeze with fear, the team catches cold. This the best way

> to create backbiting. If you see anger in the team, it is because of fear. If they are fearful, then it's because you are. You will know this is true when you get angry, when you see them get angry. Your role is to calm their fears with your passion, mission, and stated vision. To lead them into battle with a confident and happy face will calm them right now.

I have come to realize that the real juice in life for me—the peace, fulfillment, and joy of my life—comes from relationships, not material gain. I know it's easy to say that. All my clients feel like, "That's great, Dan, and I think I believe you, but give me the money first, then I can discover for myself that you are right."

There is nothing wrong with money, until it rises to the number-one position in your life. It is the false god that is so appealing at first, but always winds up being so empty. I once felt as if material gain would provide freedom and offer peace. That was the biggest lie I ever bought into.

I have coached quite a few CEOs who have achieved massive success but don't change who they are. They see money as offering essentially two valuable things: freedom and memories. With money you have the freedom of time to create memories with the people you love. Unfortunately, I have also coached a handful of CEOs who achieved massive success while guzzling their own Kool-Aid and reading their own press releases. Pride rose and their lives fell.

Think about money for a moment. I want you to have tons of it. I don't want it to take over your life and change you. It needn't do so. When you look deeply at money, why do people want it? They want financial freedom to stop worrying and have the time to go and create memories.

But what can happen after you make a ton of money? You worry about the tax consequences. Then you have to hire a financial advisor who asks you for lots of documents, and then you have to make decisions on how you want to balance stocks, bonds, gold, and real estate investments. Do you want high risk/high reward or more conservative and safe, while you watch your friends make a boat load of money on that high flying new play where they got in on the ground floor? How much time do you want to spend networking to find the investments you want to make?

Your worries will not go away when you are rich. But they can diminish today. You can find almost everything you want that you believe riches can bring you, today. Why not have peace, joy, satisfaction, fulfillment, a great relationship with the love of your life today, and then still get the money as icing on the cake?

13

FROM THE SUITE TO THE SWAMP

I still remember the heady dot-com era. The only trouble I faced back then was managing an exploding business. It was euphoric. My inventory was time, and since I couldn't create more time, I had to follow the laws of supply and demand and kept increasing my rates. I never wanted to tell a prospect no, so I would regulate my availability by pricing.

When I was out of time (can't put hours in the day), I would raise my rate for all my clients. A couple would drop off making room for a couple of new ones, all at the higher price. I was fair, however; so when my fee went up for a new client, all my client fees went up. When my fee for a new client went down, all my clients enjoyed the reduction in price. My fee peaked at $5,800 per session, and sessions were reduced to one and a half hours. This went on for about three years, but didn't last.

In 2000, the dot-com bubble burst. Start-ups burned through their money at a startling rate. There was no venture capital available. Companies who were not at breakeven yet just ran out of money and couldn't raise more. During the early years of the crash, Silicon Valley lost 367,000 jobs. My client base went down, as well as my rate. I was happy to have seven CEOs to coach at $2,800 per session.

Instead of working with clients on passion and boldness like I had been doing for the previous four years, and creating an aggressive strategy, I was now coaching CEOs on how to quash fear and navigate RIFs (reduction in force, aka layoffs) with as much love as possible. Our strategy was no longer how to manage explosive growth but how to manage the cash reserves to hang on long enough to survive. It was about maintaining a positive attitude while treading water in a cesspool.

I worked steadily with my clients to help them maintain the highest possible levels of passion to move past their own fears and lead their teams with as much optimism as we could create. In fact, I learned a ton about the emotion of fear during those years. In that new space of business retraction, I was lost again. And this was perfect, because I got to look at the fundamentals of building real businesses on real value again, and how to help others (and myself) deal with fear. I wouldn't trade what I learned during the dot-com era or the crash, not for anything.

Where were you when the dot-com bust happened? The crash happened in 2000–2001. If you were born in 1988, you would have been thirteen years old. No memory of it I am sure. But today you would be thirty-one. So if you were not here living through the dot-com era and subsequent bust, I need to tell you about it, so the next one doesn't hit you unprepared. And I want you prepared. I don't see anything like the dot-com bust on the horizon, but I always remind myself that the tide does go out, it doesn't always come in.

At the start of the dot-com era, the market was on fire like I had never seen before. Money was "free" for start-ups. You could raise investment money on almost any idea you pitched if it was around the internet. Venture capitalists focused on flipping or selling their start-up companies after only six months. You didn't need a market or sales; in fact, you didn't even need a finished product. You just needed a compelling product idea and a team that was starting work on it.

Back then the VCs told me that, in the sales valuation, each engineer on the staff of a new company was worth $6 million. If the CEO told the board he or she needed four engineers, the board would tell them to hire twelve. This was because of the valuation they brought, not the need for engineering talent. But engineers were nearly impossible to find. They were all happily employed.

In one instance, I watched a board authorize buying, not leasing, brand-new BMW 325i's as a signing bonus for any engineer who would agree to come work for the company. It was the Wild West meets the Gold Rush, on acid.

Then it hit.

The IPOs of internet companies emerged with ferocity and frequency, sweeping the nation up in euphoria. Investors were blindly grabbing every new issue without even looking at the business plan to find out, for example, how long the company would take before making a profit, if ever. Obviously, this made no sense. The first shots through this bubble came from the companies themselves; many reported huge losses, and some folded outright within months of their offering.

Siliconaires were moving out of $4 million estates and back to the room above their parents' garage. In the year 1999, there were 457 IPOs, most of which were internet and technology related. Of those 457 IPOs, 117 doubled in price on the first day of trading. In 2001 the number of IPOs dwindled to 76, few of them were tech related, and none of them doubled on the first day.

We were all lost.

I was at the top cruising speed of my career. I was wanted by a lot of CEOs and paid extremely well. It felt like I had mastered this craft and was now reaping the rewards. But then on one fateful morning, everything changed.

I had just driven across the Dumbarton Bridge over San Francisco Bay on a bright sunny morning in March 2000. I was eagerly looking forward to facilitating an executive team's offsite strategy meeting for one of my many client companies.

The market was roaring, and the room at the Palo Alto Hyatt was packed with excitement and back slapping. The company had filed their S-1 form to go out with an IPO on the NASDAQ. We were all excited to dive into a strategic planning session based on what to do after the IPO and how to spend all those millions of dollars that were sure to come home from New York within two months. There were big plans and bubbling excitement in the room. Each of the twelve VPs in the room could taste the wealth and their imminent transformation into millionaires.

At about 10:00 that morning, Dave got a note. He quickly walked out of the room. I was worried that it was a medical emergency with a family member. But I was up in front leading, so I proceeded without hesitation to keep up the strategy session for the next twenty minutes.

When Dave returned to the training room, his face was ashen. He motioned for me to stop and gave everyone a twenty-minute break. As the two of us left the room, Dave told me Goldman Sachs was pulling his IPO offering. The company was not going public.

All that morning, protected in a hotel training room, no one was aware that the NASDAQ had just crashed. By the time Dave and I spoke, the market had lost over 600 points and was racing to the bottom. Dave asked me what I thought we should do. I told him that we needed to be honest and forthright about the news. We should chat for thirty minutes openly, to give the individuals a few moments to swallow the devastating news. Then we should pivot at once.

I said, "This market signal doesn't look good at all. I have been worried about this crazy market for a while. It's been off the hook with speculation. Because this is such a huge correction, this may not end soon. Let's spend the rest of the day working on a new contingency strategy of cost cutting as deeply as we can in case we have to, in order to weather out this storm."

That day, in that conference room, we went from how to manage a corporate hiring strategy of sixty new employees and massive expansion, to which employees should be included in the first possible RIF of thirty people. The new goal for the offsite abruptly changed from how to invest the spoils of massive victory, to rationing food and water for survival.

WHEN THE PATH SHIFTS

That was one of my most difficult days of coaching. Clearly we experienced a shift in the market that registered a 9 on the economic Richter scale. In the space of five minutes, every executive in the room went from flying high, seeing the finish line of personal wealth, to staring into the grim reality of firing employees and hunkering down for an unprecedented storm.

They were having a hard time with the abrupt shift in emotion, and most were scared half to death on how to lead the rest of the organization through this crisis. (BTW, the company did survive and eventually achieved a successful IPO a few years later. They were one of very few who made it out of the storm intact.)

My heart was shattered for this team. Men and women who had worked sixty- to eighty-hour weeks for years, with their hopes and dreams standing at the doorstep, realized that not only was their dream dashed, but they also had to lay off people who had struggled alongside them.

The problem for me was that I couldn't feel the sadness and disappointment that was blanketing me. I had a job to do. My job was to pull them forward to address what was before them, but on the way home, I cried.

We can suddenly be lost all over again. I love that I got to enjoy the dot-com bubble, and I am even more grateful for what I learned during the crash. I am a better coach because of both.

Do remember that most millennials and all of Gen Z employees (born between 1995 and 2015) have no personal experience with the dot-com bubble or crash. And you get to lead them without this wisdom-generating experience.

Most of us begin our careers not certain of our path—we are all essentially lost. When we think we finally found it, the darn thing shifts again, the path turns, a new path is revealed. Life is littered with discovery, surprises, disappointments, and great blessings. All of this is the natural journey of life, and so it's natural and even okay to become lost over and over again.

The idea is to maintain your passion and stay foolish, like Steve Jobs tells us, regardless of what's going on around you. Sometimes we actually need an earthquake in our lives to get us off autopilot to force us to reconsider what is important and to discover anew what we want in our lives. Our hopes and dreams will change, but I believe you can find the core of what you want to deliver into the world with your effort and career. We constantly get to shift ourselves to something new and find our passion all over again. If we are ready for change, it's easier for us to embrace the rushes and crashes and take them in stride.

Here is a trick I developed on how you can find your heart's desire and calm the noise of the analytical mind. The other day I was in a seminar. One of the exercises was to find and articulate what we wanted to create in our life. The purpose was to help us identify our heartfelt calling.

The man next to me was my assigned buddy, Abraham. He was stuck. He said he was moved by two things, not just one. One was coaching lacrosse, which he loved, and the other was to support a nonprofit that helped kids, which he also loved. He just couldn't choose which he loved more. After a few moments I pulled a quarter out of my pocket. I flipped the coin in the air, caught it, and quickly slapped it onto the back of my other hand, keeping the coin covered.

"Lacrosse is heads, the nonprofit is tails." I pretended to privately peek at the result of the coin toss. Then I looked him in the eye and asked, "Which one do you hope it is, heads or tails?"

He called, "Heads." I quickly and carefully removed the coin from the back of my hand, so he couldn't see the result, and put it back into my pocket. He looked at me with that question in his eyes, "Well what was it?"

I said we don't make major life decisions on a coin toss. It really doesn't matter how the coin toss came out. When it got down to having to decide, the heart spoke. What matters is that your heart rendered up your answer to what you really wanted, and that is to coach lacrosse. Your heart knows what you want. But it will only tell you when you get out of your head.

He laughed and said, "Oh that's good. That's good."

We get to get out of our heads and find what our hearts want. That is where our passion lies. It's really hard to find and continue to follow our calling. But it's worth it. Your calling is where your greatest joy meets the world's greatest need.

Wait. What if there is no being lost? What if our life is perfect as a messy journey? Even the pain is perfect. The pain, frustration, and endless trials and errors of life are guideposts turning us left and then right to find our calling. What is perfect are the life lessons that will serve us on our journey, a journey through life in a world that is in a constant state of change.

At sixteen, I got a job at a Mobile gas station. I was a gas station attendant. What if I loved that job? I loved meeting people, of being of service to an elderly woman on a rainy day. I loved to ask her, "Fill it with premium?" She might say, "No, just give me ten dollars of regular." So I would wash her windshield and check her oil and even the pressure in her tires. At the end, I would come to her window and hand her the credit card slip for her to sign.

That world doesn't exist anymore. If my calling was to be the best gas station attendant, I couldn't do that anymore. We are always lost, and since life is a journey where everything changes all the time, I guess I now realize that I was never lost. I was just on my journey. And every bit of it was, in fact, perfect.

What is your calling? If you could do anything and be guaranteed to not fail, what would you go for? Look into your heart and find what is most important to you. Dare to get on your journey and dig to find out what's in your heart. Go, try, and fail. Find success and breakdown. This is your journey. And it doesn't get any better than truly being on your journey, out of your head.

TAKEAWAYS

- We need to learn from the dot-com bubble and the burst. The tide doesn't always come in, and it doesn't always go out.
- Learn how to handle sudden and tragic news in the business environment. The key is to embrace the black and white of the event and immediately get onto the solution. Don't get stuck in the bad news.
- Your subconscious mind already knows what you really want. It's just the conscious mind that gets in the way. Use the coin toss trick to find out what you really want.

14

"YOUR EGO IS NOT YOUR AMIGO"

"Your ego is not your amigo." That was a memorable line from Mark Wahlberg in the film *Mile 22*.

What is the ego? The psychoanalytical definition is "the part of the mind that mediates between the conscious and the unconscious and is responsible for reality testing and a sense of personal identity."

This definition leads us to believe ego is something that tries to find balance. Do not think too low of yourself, and do not think too highly of yourself. The universal problem with the ego begins when, usually out of fear, we inflate our ego and stop reality testing. We are attempting to overcompensate for what we fearfully perceive is going to happen. We compensate in the ego in many different forms.

As humans we are excellent at reading the authenticity of others' egos. When it comes to others, we can see if we are reading an overcompensation, which causes us to reluctantly follow the leader not quite as closely.

A healthy ego is fine for setting boundaries against abuse, a feeling of self-worth, and an internal belief in your innate ability to contribute to the world. A healthy ego enables you to say, "I get to win at life also."

But when the ego gets overinflated, it's devastating to relationships. An inflated ego is self-will run riot. Unchecked ego can destroy everything and everyone in its path. I have found in working with thousands of executives that a vast majority of the time an overinflated ego and pride are rooted in the foundation of low self-esteem—often from previous wounds caused by others. These previous wounds are often found in the person's early years of life.

This overcompensation technique of bravado and inflated ego can work to a point. It is seen in the demanding and demeaning boss. And if the leader happens to strike it rich quickly, the team can see the inflated ego as a symbol of supreme confidence. But over the long haul, which is what massive success takes, ego never works. It doesn't work because relationships are abused, and people with healthy self-esteem simply will not work over the long haul with someone who puts them down.

I have focused my writing on many of the success stories with clients over the years, but my track record, while very good, is not without failures.

Kirk was in a vulnerable place when he admitted that he was pondering having an affair. He had already emotionally left his marriage; the only thing left was the physical consummation with this new woman. He asked me my opinion.

I pointed out that it was not my job to be his moral compass, but that said, I described the pain and cost of such a move as I have experienced it. It is difficult to see the total cost through the lens of infatuation, but the costs are real, long-lasting, and painful.

I listed the likely outcomes of an affair followed by a likely divorce:

- The intense emotional damage to his children (he had two).
- The financial cost of paying upward of $30k per month, for ten years, in alimony and child support.
- The tremendous weight of the emotional baggage he was about to pick up and drag behind himself for decades.
- The impact to him around times like Thanksgiving, children's birthdays, and weddings from damaged extended family ties.
- Finally, the dividing of friends. You will lose more than half if

you are the one initiating the divorce. How will it feel to walk into the restaurant with your new wife only to meet two couple friends from the old marriage? It's just painful and awkward.
- My experience with people shows that most affairs do not render lasting romantic relationships.

Kirk listened and nodded that he understood.

I felt I knew what this conversation meant. I didn't see Kirk again for several months. Kirk decided to take a break from coaching. But one day I ran into him while attending a conference as I was walking down the hallway on the fourth floor of the hotel. When Kirk, leaving his room with new girlfriend in tow, came out of their room to join me in the elevator, he nodded and even introduced me. I smiled and was gracious because I don't judge, and I still love Kirk. It was just awkward for them.

When I was working with Kirk, he was an up-and-coming rock star in the high-tech community. But the years rolled by and I lost touch with him. Every now and then a client would tell me something about Kirk's life today. I miss Kirk and would love to sit and visit with him, but he is unwilling.

OVERCOMPENSATION BY WORK

Consider another CEO, Thomas. He had a warrior's heart for success and was a self-proclaimed workaholic. As CEO he held executive team offsites on Saturday and Sunday. He put in sixty- to eighty-hour work-weeks and demanded the same of all those around him. Thomas was on the path to success. The team was making remarkable progress.

I worked with Thomas and his team for about six months. Thomas felt the leadership training was effective but now done, so he cut my firm out of the budget. All of this was fine as far as I was concerned, but I worried and told him that this pace could not endure. Theirs was a plan of single-minded purpose, and this intensity worked for the next couple years, but as great as intensity is for a sprint, it will not work for a marathon. And building a business from scratch toward a liquidity event is almost always a marathon.

As you would expect, the pace quickly burned out the team. Irritability set in. The cycle of success simply created more intensity and push for more. Finally, a business setback, the loss of a critical customer. It was to become the first of many setbacks, mostly because Thomas couldn't handle a failure of any kind.

But Thomas's pride and ego only made the trials a new reason to double down on effort and commitment. Soon the members of the executive team started leaving. Maybe it was the pressure from home, or the lack of any job satisfaction, but they began to find other positions. In a crushing blow, Thomas's own board let him go.

Pride and ego prevented Thomas from learning from experience. Thomas did find work again, but a lot of broken glass littered his path as he scrambled to prove to the world that he was a successful man.

There may be twenty such stories in my portfolio of 4,500 clients. Still, even those few are difficult for me emotionally to remember.

Confidence coupled with humility is the key. You can and must be certain that you know how to succeed with the help of others. If you show fear, no one will want to follow you. But you don't have to have all the answers. You just need to show the courage and compassion to your team so that success will occur.

And the most important ingredient is of course love. Confident, humble, and loving is the secret recipe. But love is first and most important. When someone knows deep in their heart that you love them, you can accidentally have a bad day, or make a major mistake, and everyone will happily forgive you.

Love creates the bond of team. It has people support one another when the setbacks occur (and they always occur). It doesn't matter what's going on in the company. If they know they are loved, even when someone is angry, they will come together and reconcile.

THE STORY OF THE HUMBLE CEO

Here's a story of a CEO who killed his pride and ego and won massive success. When I sat with Mario, he told me pride and ego will kill a company. I asked him to explain.

He told me that pride and ego stand in the way of course correction, which translates to delay and costs lots of money. I asked him to give me an example.

Mario said, "Okay, there was a time not so long ago that I stood before the team at an all-hands meeting and told them that I killed our code-named Bluewater project today. That it became apparent to me last week that the product fit would just not work for the market. The timing wasn't right, and the product would not be virally embraced. I told them that it cost the company $9 million of wasted development time, as well as the lost opportunity to have created something else. As of today, I have killed all work on the project. And I am sorry to all of you. Bluewater was my idea."

Wow. That was vulnerable and courageous of him.

"No," he said, "it's selfish. If I am willing to state this publicly to my team, I just made it okay for them to do the same. Now we don't waste time or money on something we come to believe is not right. This practice ignites honesty in ourselves and with each other."

When I was meeting with Mario, his stock was trading at $4 a share. Today it's trading at $160 per share.

Please understand this fact. I know of many CEOs who had inflated pride and ego. They had success, then found success again because people were willing to work with them for a while thinking that this rock star will lead them to riches. Many of them are very successful today, even though there is a lot of wreckage in their past. They are not happy, joyous, peaceful, or fulfilled. But the common saying is, "It's easier to cry in your Porsche than on a bicycle in the rain."

My commitment and strong knowing is that you can have both: a financially success life with a rich and full heart.

TAKEAWAYS

- Your ego is the awareness and representation you hold of self.
- An overinflated ego is often caused by low self-esteem, which is rooted in old emotional wounds.
- An overinflated ego can cause us to make poor decisions, which lead to massive pain.
- The ego wants to maintain control of your life. When it sees that you are off track, it will double down with stories and denials and lean on pride to push harder to make sure the ego was right about its place in your mind.
- The key goals to focus on are confidence, humility, and love. And love is the most important, because it makes you focus on others, which puts pride and ego into the shadows of your awareness.
- The killing of pride and overinflated ego brings about cultural honesty. This leads to quick corrections and saves time and money.

15

THE REAL COST OF BURNOUT AND BLIND SPOTS

You have a dream. You have uncovered your passion. You have made a commitment to accomplish what you set out to do. Your dream now owns you, not the other way around. It doesn't feel like work anymore—you're on a joyful mission. You apply yourself to the tasks at hand. You may be putting in ten to twelve hours a day and loving every minute. You are in the zone or the flow. You are beginning to see traction toward your dream, and you want to put in more energy to watch your dream grow.

But one day someone points out to you that you were a little short with them in your response.

You immediately explain, "Oh I am sorry, but we have so much to do. We need to get X done by Friday. I am so glad you stopped by. Could you help me with this piece of the puzzle?" You didn't really even hear them. You are completely focused on getting things done, because you are passionate, and every moment feeds the glorious momentum.

In the zone, you don't even realize that you haven't spent any time with your family or friends. You haven't had fun in weeks, or even months.

You believe, "When I am done with this part, we will take a little time and go have fun."

But you don't notice that the joy and excitement of accomplishing work is slowly diminishing. The passion is leaving, replaced by increasing commitment. Work is becoming all about the end goal, no longer about the joy of the journey. You are still insanely productive, but the joy is gone, and you are slowly losing collaborators in your mission.

You finally reach a place where you feel like this: "Who cares about joy, it's all about the commitment to the goal. We are so close." You tell yourself and your loved ones that once the goal is achieved, you will have time to reconnect with them. You remind them that you are sacrificing for the good of the family. "I am doing this for you."

But in reality, you are not.

You have a new idol that comes before God and your family. That idol is your goal. Being passionately committed and focused is admirable, but not at the cost of friends and family, because we remember that everything you want in life comes from relationships.

The evolution of burnout and the blind spots that follow can take a couple of months or a couple of years to manifest. You treat nurturing relationships as a nuisance and think of them as just time away from the ultimate goal. You stop seeing friends; you may even ignore your family.

Another insidious side effect of your burning out is that you become unapproachable. People will see that you are busy, committed, and on an uninterruptible mission, which prevents them from disturbing you to ask questions or tell you about their obstacles. They would love to run something by you for your input or approval, but instead they tiptoe past your closed office door and make the decision on their own.

Sometimes their decision, without your input, is not the best solution, which forces you to step in and clean up the mess. This frustrates you even more. Because if they had just asked you, the time to repair would have been avoided. Maybe now you can begin to see the downward spiral in productivity and effectiveness and the complete collapse made possible because of broken relationships. You always have time for people. You can tell them, "I only have ten minutes, but in those ten minutes I am completely yours. How can I help?"

NEVER SAW IT COMING

The first big problem with burnout is that we can't see it coming. We have this huge blind spot that prevents us from seeing this killer. It's easier to spot burnout in others. You recognize the symptoms: A colleague is curt with their answers, cuts people off in conversations, has no joy on their face, is easily angered, and incredibly busy while focused on their goals. These are all signs of burnout.

Maybe someone will cautiously suggest the colleague take some time off. Or a friend will ask if they've had any fun lately.

Maybe you've heard these suggestions yourself. If you have, that is your notice and the only one you will get. Very few people will have the courage to confront a prickly pear cactus with a comment like, "You are burning out man. You have got to take some time off. You are becoming a pain to be around."

They know your response will be something like, "Are you crazy? Do you have any idea of what I need to get done by the end of this month?"

I have seen this hundreds of times, and in hindsight I can now see this in myself. Yes, I have burned out, and, no, I couldn't see it coming. I mean, I really didn't have a clue. It put a wet blanket on many of my relationships, which later took real effort to rebuild, and some never got rebuilt.

Another devastating effect of burnout, at least in my experience, is that I lost all joy in my work. My whole focus was on the goal, not on the journey. My days blurred into one another. It felt like I was a hamster on a nicely greased wheel.

I told myself that the end goal would be worth the sacrifice, any sacrifice, that I was making. It was a quest, a compulsion, and I was going to see it through. I assured everyone that all this immediate sacrifice was required today to build the life I was shooting for tomorrow.

The major problem is not realizing that tomorrow never comes. Being focused and driven, at the cost of relationships, becomes a new way of being. Each new day is just another day. We continue to mortgage today for the payoff tomorrow, never realizing that sacrificing today actually prevents tomorrow from ever being realized. It is this context, or way of being, that shoots the future in the foot.

In the final analysis, what we lose today in burnout, we lose in relationships that could actually help us achieve future goals. It is a lose/lose/lose scenario.

Usually burnout can only be realized by sifting through the ashes of destruction after burnout has taken its course. Usually the effects of burnout have to be so large and devastating that it becomes unavoidable to not see. Burnout causes destruction like job loss, client loss, or losing precious direct reports. Often, destruction occurs because you have accidentally killed your own dream.

Even in this final circumstance many people just become bitter about the failure and blame others. They refuse to embrace the fact that the problem was them. This scenario really breaks my heart because these were people with great promise. They had a vision, were filled with passion, made commitments, and were gaining real traction toward their dreams.

The worst days of my coaching career occur when a client does burn out and loses their job or their marriage because of it. It is hell to try to be responsible for someone else's success, to be paid for that purpose, and to see them crash and burn anyway. I have to remember my codependency training. I can offer help, but it's their life. I can be honest, and loving, and direct, but it's their decision.

I have experienced crushing remorse when, a handful of times, I read an email from a client announcing that his board just fired him. Or even worse, when a client goes dark, not taking my calls, emails, or texts. Fortunately, these instances are rare. But these are the lowest points of my life, because they deal with someone I desperately care about. I can't take responsibility for someone else's life. I get it. But be a coach and enroll yourself authentically in the life of another person, then let me know how easy it is to compartmentalize. Fortunately, this situation has happened only a handful of times in my career. No one has ever blamed me for their failure, but I sure have.

On the other side, once you've hit bottom and start to work your way back, help will appear, often from surprising places and people.

I reached a dark point of burnout in my own life, and when I got back on my feet, I called up one of my old clients, Alex, and just told him my whole story. I didn't even know what kind of reaction I would get from him, but I had to be honest.

His response floored me. "Oh my gosh, I had no idea what happened to you. I am so sorry that you went through that. Let's make an appointment right now to reengage."

And just like that, I was back in business. Even at the time, I knew it wasn't that he desperately needed my coaching. He was becoming a client again for my sake. That was one of the most loving acts anyone has ever done for me.

Alex was the first of several who came back as clients after I told them the story of my divorce and search for myself again. They all came back for me, but clearly not for what they could get from me.

After a few years my clients keep me because of what I now bring, which is enormously more than before. What I went through brings tremendous depth and humility to my work that I never had before. Now my work is completely about them, and nothing about me.

But I will never forget my previous clients' compassion and kindness to let me be humble, share my story, and still want to help me back up by reengaging with me as a coach.

I want to share what a couple of my clients have said, so you might grasp for a moment how great it is to be in a position to coach others. It warms my humble heart to hear that one of my VP clients was once trying to explain to a director-level report who I was and what I do. The director had asked who I was, because he had been seeing me in the building a lot.

The VP was stumbling while trying to help the director understand emotional quotient coaching, which is experiential, not just intellectual learning. Another VP I coach who was walking by at the time and heard the conversation stepped in and said, "Let me put it this way, if it wasn't for Dan Foxx, we wouldn't be here as a company." Oh, melt me.

Then another C-level report, during a conversation with the CEO, was asked, "You have done so much for the company recently, what do you need from me?"

He answered, "Well I guess now would be the time to ask for a raise, but honestly I don't need one. What I want is your commitment that you will never stop letting me work with Dan Foxx."

Okay, now I was completely slain. I don't see myself like that. But it still warms my heart.

The best test to see if you are suffering from burnout—and to actually see through the blind spot—is to check in to see if your passion is still rooted and you feel a sense of joy as you pursue your dreams. Check in often.

TAKEAWAYS

- We have a natural blind spot so we can't see our burnout.
- Burnout causes us to become self-centered and not good listeners at all, unapproachable.
- Our human connection suffers, including our family.
- Burnout unchecked often leads to a personal crash, but that is therapeutic, not fun. Afterward, you challenge your focus and goals and often recenter your work/life balance, maybe for the first time in your life.

16

SUCCESS IS A MARATHON, NOT A SPRINT

First, some financial background: When you start a high-tech company, you usually need to raise money. Much of that money is derived from venture capital firms (VCs). They have portfolios, which are a collection of companies they invest in. Usually the portfolio for the venture capital firm ages to maybe seven years, and then the limited investors to the VC firm start getting an itch to see a handsome return on their investment.

If you raise VC money, everyone will expect a liquidity event to get their cash and profit out. A liquidity event can occur when you take a company stock public, called an IPO, or it can be in the form of selling the company to an equal sized or larger entity, which is called an M/A or merger/acquisition.

Many of these parent companies are already trading on a stock exchange. In this latter instance, the seller is usually paid with some combination of stock and cash. But at least the stock of the parent company is liquid on the NASDAQ or Dow, so it can be converted into cash right away. These investors do not want you to build a happy and successful business that will still be privately held and growing for twenty years. They are investing in a future liquidity event. This means that if you have to raise money in the traditional high-tech world, sometime in the next few years you are going to be bought or go public.

Indulge me. Here are some numbers: In the report *Initial Public Offerings: Median Age of IPOs Through 2015*, Professor J. R. Ritter states that from 1980 until 2015 there were 8,178 IPOs. The average age of a company that went IPO was eight years.

I am not going to include the outliers to my conversation—those few companies that rocket with viral growth but have never made a profit but go public in just a couple of years. We are discussing the norm.

Naturally, starting a company demands passion and excitement from the CEO on down. But remember, you are beginning a marathon, not a sprint. How will you maintain your high level of passion and commitment while keeping yourself reenergized to fuel the necessary creativity over eight years?

Certainly, you realize that there will be long periods of heavy slogging that will make you question why you started the company in the first place. You'll have difficult days and unexpected downturns in the market or your industry. How about those unpleasant surprises and setbacks? These realities can wear you down over a period of time. Think of the raindrop on the forehead as torture. The first drop of water on your head is nothing. But sixteen hours of drip, drip, drip can drive you crazy.

What's the answer to maintaining your high level of passion and commitment to reenergizing yourself? It is to make sure that you check in with yourself and have fun along the way. Be mindful. Bring mental attention back to the present moment. Ask how you are going to create fun today, so you can find the desire and energy to press on. And make sure that you maintain a healthy work/life balance so you don't burn out.

Do a joy check. Check the level of joy in your life every week. This is not for the purpose of self-indulgence. It is to see if you will have the stamina through work/life balance and joy to want to continue for the long haul.

When I work with a client facing burnout, I often ask, "How long do you feel you can go at this pace? Now really think about it. I know you are racing to a finish, the liquidity event. But how many days, weeks, or months can you just hang on and endure feeling the way you do today?"

Many of my clients answer honestly. "Maybe six months to a year."

Then I ask, "So when you look at your crystal ball, how long do you think it will take on your current trajectory to reach a liquidity event?"

They usually answer two to three years. I ask them if they can see the obvious disconnect between how long they can hang on versus how long it will take to get to the finish line. They will be over before the game is. It is insane to play a game like this because of longevity; you can't win.

I also ask, "Oh, by the way, do you think you can win when your leadership reflects how much you are downtrodden and burned out? Wouldn't winning require you to be inspirational for the team?"

The answer is to plan for success with a set date in mind, as if you could control it. Then work in such a way that you enjoy life, who you work with, and what you are up to, so that you can say, "I am having so much fun, I could do this forever."

Here is the paradox. On the one hand, you want to create a work/life where you could go on forever; however, you also know that some unknown clock is ticking and the company needs to show viral top-line revenue growth, with a path to a consistent, profitable ROI. We can't love our job and companies so much we'd be happy to stay with the company for twenty years; investors will not wait that long. But we also can't play all out and sprint when it will take three years to reach real execution traction. We must balance between the two.

I have seen really smart CEOs work themselves into the ground because of their own impatience for a liquidity event. They not only start to burn out, they also start making mistakes; they become irritable with their boards, the members of which are also focused on the liquidity event. As a result, the original CEO is replaced by a new CEO.

I have also seen CEOs who were jogging not sprinting in their play and were caught off guard by a restless board that decided that the time to get out is now. They feel that without passion and viral growth, the company will never get more successful than it is now.

Okay, so what do we do? The first thing is to accept that success will take some time, often a long time. If you are just starting a company, it may take a decade to reach massive success. The years may be a bit fewer in high tech, but not by that much. Get your mind around the idea that this is going to be a long haul. This should cause you to check and see if the industry, product, and market will excite you for years to come.

Don't go into a company where you don't really like the space or product, just because you think you might get an IPO or M/A payday in a couple of years. The bet is not a good one. You want to plan and work to create success as soon as possible so you are not just trudging through the mud slowly. This kind of attitude will get you killed by the competition who is waking up in the morning wanting to eat raw meat. Yours.

Instead, work and plan quickly and efficiently, but plan and adjust your attitude that it may take a long time.

Next you need to remember that because this race is a marathon and not a sprint, it will be important to set your pace for water breaks and rest. Water breaks might be committing to be home at say 7:00 p.m. every night. That's every night with only two or three exceptions per year. Rest is taking a vacation.

You will have to be rigorous with yourself. I have told clients who are on the edge of burnout that I want their commitment to be home at 6:00 p.m. every night for the next six months. They come in as early as they want, but they have to be turning the handle of the front door by 6:00 p.m., hell or high water.

In addition, I ask for their commitment to leave the cell phone and laptop in the trunk of the car, locked up. If there's an emergency, coworkers have your home landline number.

I don't know, but I believe that a few marriages have been saved by this practice. How does this advice relate to business coaching? It can save you $10,000 to $20,000 a month in child support and alimony, plus the avoidance of picking up a lot of emotional baggage that will not serve you in your next play. And you avoid pain.

The other benefit, which is huge, is that you gain perspective. When you make it a point to walk away for a night or a weekend, you come back to the company's issues with a fresh new perspective. When this happens, you find the creative solutions you really need. Those creative solutions would have never come through if you were staring at the computer screen all night.

YOU HAVE FIRST-WORLD PROBLEMS

In spring 2019, I called an Uber ride to my Orlando hotel. The driver was pleasant. He looked like he was a professional of some kind. He spoke with a Spanish accent. On the ride to the hotel I asked him where he was born and raised.

"I was born in Venezuela and lived there all my life."

"When did you come to Orlando?"

"I came here last year."

"Welcome. What did you do in Venezuela?"

"I was a producer of a television show in Caracas."

"Wow, that sounds great. What brought you here?"

"One of our news broadcasts kind of put down the current leader, Maduro. The next day the troops came into the station and killed several of our employees. Many more were arrested and taken away. I happened to be out of the building at the time and heard about what was happening. I went home, got my wife and daughter, and we immediately went to the airport. Fortunately, I had some money and credit cards, so we caught a flight to Florida. As far as I know everyone in the television station was killed, arrested, or on the run. They closed the station down."

"Oh my gosh. I am so sorry to hear that. Are you and your family okay now?"

"We are fine. I don't know about my extended family's safety. I really appreciate America. I am so glad my family and I are alive. My only regret is that we left our two cars, house, and all our belongings there. We just ran away. You Americans have it so great here."

"I know. You are right. Welcome to our country. I love that you are embracing our nation and making a living for yourself and your family."

"It's not my profession, but I get to work all night driving people. I am hoping it will be a busy night."

How would our attitude change if we took a few minutes each week and just looked at our freedoms and opportunities?

Let me ask you, the reader, a few questions:

- Do you have food today?
- Do you have a job?
- Do you have a car, with fuel in the tank?
- Can you say anything publicly without fear?
- Do you have at least one friend you can confide in?
- Do you have freedom to travel anyplace in the country you want and do any job you want to go after?
- Do you have basic healthcare?

If you answered yes to most of those questions, you have it made compared to much of the planet. Count your blessings daily. It will bring perspective to your life. It will make your problems seem really small. You will find more gratitude, more joy, and more peace in your life. When you have those, you will create better relationships, have more creativity, and possess more passion, which leads you to a place where life is worth living. It is easy to create relationships, or build on the ones we have when we are feeling grateful. There is something attractive about being around happy people.

The vast majority of us are facing first-world problems, not third-world problems. In our privileged world we have the luxury of making mountains out of mole hills.

Most people wait to feel the emotion of gratitude before they express gratitude. We think that gratitude is an action that follows feeling. That's backward. Actually, once we decide to be grateful and express gratitude, especially when we don't feel like it, the warmth of feeling grateful will emerge. Said in another way, gratefulness is an action followed by the feeling.

In business, we tend to only focus on what is wrong in our team and the company. We worry out loud about what is wrong with the market, the customers, and some members of our team, which leads to feelings of victimization, resentment, and sadness. In this state of being morose, we create no relationships. We don't inspire anyone. And we create results that are dull and broken. People want to work and be around people where they feel wanted and appreciated. Gratefulness brings that to the table.

Success is a place you come from, not a place you get to. Success and happiness is, to a great degree, an inside job. Gain some new perspective. You probably really do have it made in this life. With some perspective, your problems are actually small, but your potential is really enormous.

TAKEAWAYS

- Success almost always takes longer than you think. So pace yourself for the long play.
- Create a small piece of fun or laughter every day.

- Check your burnout meter. How long do you really think it will take to create the success you dream of? Then ask yourself how long you can go on the way you are before you get fed up and quit or get fired. If your answer to the first question is longer in time than the second, then you are playing a game you cannot win.
- Demand discipline of yourself to have work/life balance. Make a commitment to a time you will be home every night. Decide how many Saturdays you are willing to work during a year. Keep track and don't go over your limit.
- Set up the game so you know you can maintain your passion and still want to play in the company, because success usually takes twice as long as you think.
- The act of gratitude leads to the feeling of being grateful.

17

IT'S ABOUT OTHERS, NOT ABOUT YOU

Your life is about relationships.

Do you want a big, full life? Then please embrace this chapter.

We are quite adept at blame. We blame others for anything and everything wrong in our world. It's seductive to absolve ourselves of responsibility and shift all the blame for our unhappiness onto others.

You want to transform the world? This is the way to do it. The principle here is to clean up your side of the street. Don't default to blame. Check your own side and make sure you aren't to blame as well. I am advising you to have no interest in whether or not the other person cleans up their side of the street. It's not your job to expect others to do anything. You apologize, or clean up your side of the street, for you, not to reconcile the relationship. It may happen that you both heal, but don't let that become part of your mission, for if you do, you may be disappointed and create a new reason to resent the other person.

Let's say two days ago a fellow employee greeted you with a hearty good morning.

Maybe you had finished a difficult call and were angry. Your response to the greeting was, "Yah, what's so good about it?" That set the ball in motion.

The greeter got hurt. They wrote a story in their head that you had a personal problem with them. Now, two days later, you are in a meeting with them, and they criticized your idea publicly. Wow, you think, that's harsh.

Now the two of you are on a roll. It is likely that you both will begin to look for any way to throw each other under the bus. But if you are completely honest, and review the most recent exchanges, you can see you had a hand in starting the negative exchanges. Once you realize you had a part in this, you can fix it.

Instead of allowing the deterioration of the relationship to escalate, you approach your recently created nemesis and explain, "You know I feel there is a problem between us. As I look back, I think I was a bit selfish and rude that morning you greeted me and I responded sarcastically because of what was going on in my life that day. I am sorry."

You really don't care if the other person even asks for forgiveness for their part. Of course, you are willing to receive their apology, but there is no expectation they will offer one. You are offering an apology for your peace of mind to be able to see yourself as a person without any blame, because you have gone and done what you can to clean up your own mess.

What about when you're completely innocent? Let's say coworker Barbara said or did something to hurt you, and after careful reflection, you can't see anything you did to contribute to the problem. It may be something that Barbara did a year ago, or ten years ago that hurt. And that hurt was real.

Since that event, you have replayed that scene of what she did over and over in your mind. Every time you replay the tape of Barbara's actions, you feel the pain all over again. The first time, when you experienced the offense, you were hurt, especially since it was all her fault. But every time you dredged up that memory of pain, it's now your fault. You brought it back up, instead of letting it go. The Latin root for *feel* is *sentire*, to sense or to feel. So resentment is to re-feel the pain.

In summary, I want you to get this. The first time you were hurt by someone, it was maybe all their fault. Shame on them. But every time you re-*sentire*, or bring up the painful memory, it's your fault.

In this last example Barbara has probably long forgotten what she did. She's not carrying any negative emotion about either you or the event. But you are still hanging on to it. Barbara is occupying a room in your head, and she's not paying rent. You have the choice to kick her out of that room. How you kick her out is through forgiveness. Only in this way can you let it go, instead of just burying it.

Let's look at this concept of forgiveness from another view. If you want to be free of the negative emotions of bitterness or resentment so you can be more positive, then you need to do something different than you have done before.

If there was a fire in your backyard and you wanted to extinguish it, what would you do? First you need to understand the nature of fire. Fire is hot and dry. You know that to extinguish it you need to apply the opposite. The opposite of a hot/dry fire is cold/wet water.

When it comes to the nature of bitterness and resentment, we need to understand the nature of it and apply the opposite. Resentment is often accompanied by a secret wish that the offender will be met with some bad luck. What would be the opposite? It would be love, and wishing them well.

But you exclaim, "I don't feel that for them. It would be hypocritical and a lie if I were to wish them well, and not mean it."

No, it wouldn't. Ongoing resentment is like drinking the poison and expecting the other person to die. Just like we don't wait for the feeling of gratefulness to be grateful, forgiveness is a decision followed by an act that ultimately renders a feeling. The most important time to forgive is when we don't feel like it. When we forgive, we then feel no resentment toward the other person, and we then feel like we wish them well. This is the path to peace and love for all others, and especially for yourself.

Sometimes the wound is so deep, or it has been there for so long, you may feel that you just can't forgive. Sometimes there are things in our life that are just too big to overcome. This is a place for professional help. But I have seen people work with professionals for years, and still not be able to overcome the negative issue.

If this discussion resonates with you about some person or event, and you can't see yourself being set free, then we get to entertain the ultimate alternative. You may be reluctant to bring the God of your understanding into the picture, and if this is the case, you can skip over the next few paragraphs. But if you are open to the idea, then I want to offer the concept and the power of prayer.

In these instances, it's important to take the greatest opposite action to resentment. That is to pray for them. Prayer is an emotional/spiritual action. And since resentment is an emotional/spiritual ailment of wishing them ill, prayer is the best solution. Pray for good things to come to them, especially when you don't feel like it. If you pray for your arch enemy every day for a month, you will find that you actually begin to feel as if you mean the prayer by the end of the month. It's not logical. It's spiritual. And it works. Remember, feelings follow actions.

If you believe there is a God, do you believe he is able and willing to forgive you? You may say, "Yes, he is able and willing, but I don't deserve his forgiveness, so I don't ask."

God's forgiveness is a gift, not something you earn. It is there for the asking. It's called grace. Grace is an undeserved gift. Maybe you don't feel you deserve to be forgiven.

Hanging on to guilt and blame has a price. That price is the loss of peace. If there are resentments and blame, there can be no reconciliation. Look at America today, or the world for that matter. This is where we are and why: "You are wrong. I am right. I blame you for all our nation's ills. You don't deserve forgiveness. I can't even talk to you, because you are the enemy."

Forgiveness is not easy. Embracing forgiveness means I no longer get to be right about how you are wrong. If I forgive, I let go of my self-righteous anger toward you. Another way of putting it is that I get to be free from all my judgments, resentments, and ill feelings, which bring me, and all my other relationships, down. Have you ever spent an hour with someone who does nothing but spew vitriol about someone else? Did you rush to be with them again? Probably not.

TAKEAWAYS

- Blame is a selfish act. Clean up your side of the street, then forgive others.
- You are the one who carries the pain of bitterness and resentment.
- Do yourself a personal favor, forgive others.
- The original pain may have been someone else's fault, but every time you remember the event, the pain you feel is your fault.
- Peace is found in forgiveness, so choose: righteous indignation or peace.
- Sometimes it takes the help of the God of your understanding.

18

WAKE UP FROM YOUR TRANCE

Do you brush your teeth before or after the shower? Regardless of which one you chose, you do this the same way every day, correct? When you fold one leg over the other, do you place your right leg over the left, or the left over the right? Right now, fold one leg over the other. Why did you put your left leg over your right, or vice versa?

Both teeth brushing and leg crossing are forms of a trance.

Which sock do you put on first, left or right? Why? You may not even know because, again, the actions are part of an autopilot trance. That's not bad. In these examples, like thousands of others, the autopilot trance creates efficiency and saves time. In these instances, there is no right or wrong; your choices have no consequences, good or bad. It is just something that needs to be done, and you do it without having to spend time thinking about it.

The whole topic of autopilot trance in this arena we can call profitable because of productive efficiency. But what about the other areas of your life? What if I say, "You may get a promotion at work"?

Is your first reaction, "Oh boy, increase in pay and more responsibility"? Or "No, I don't want that responsibility and to have to work with those peers"?

How about, "Our company is going to launch a new product, and we think you are the right person to lead this endeavor"? To which you respond, "Great, thank you." Or "OMG total fear. What if I don't succeed?"

We have a context that we come from when we face anything that involves change. Where we come from drives our response to everything. This context has formed and been built over decades. These auto-responses are so natural. They help us immediately write a story that validates our auto-response. In these instances, can you see that if you operate on autopilot and auto-response, you really don't have a choice? Is your past and the trance making the decisions for you?

Are you living in a trance? I will say to a great degree you are. Let me explain. As you look back over yesterday, do you feel like you were operating in freedom of choice, or did you respond somewhat automatically, without really thinking through all the options? Did you do what you did on purpose, or was it reactionary? Did you have an immediate reaction to an idea, or were you open and contemplative, even in the face of your first response? Or did you exercise real choice after contemplation and do what you know would have been best to do or say, regardless of your first autopilot reaction?

Do you ever find yourself in a meeting and notice that you are in a dazed or muted condition? Like all you can do is just sit and listen. You have no interest in raising your hand and speaking your authentic truth, knowing it may fly in the face of consensus.

Do you find yourself just going through the motions in an unconscious, cataleptic, or hypnotic condition? Are you aware that you are checked out? In this state are you aware that you do not exercise the freedom of choice? Have you ever heard someone in the organization say, "That's just the way we have always done it"?

Now these descriptions may seem extreme, but is there any truth in them for you? Have you experienced similar autopilot for hours or days in your life? Me too. But now I notice it, sometimes a little late, but I notice it, so I can change. I want to live my life on purpose, not on autopilot. I want to be present and aware of my thoughts and actions. I want to live life on purpose and with choice. I want to question my first responses.

Why is this relevant? Because it is critical to change the context of how we live life in order to be able to create a new one. I am speaking of creating a life truly worth living. For example, because we are living in somewhat of a trance, we are completely unaware that our vision of the future is almost completely viewed through the lens of our past. Some call that wisdom; some just assume that what worked in the past will work again in the present and in the future.

Yes, as we make decisions going forward, our past experiences/wisdom can help us avoid mistakes. But our past also dictates what we believe is possible in the future. And that is incredibly limiting. If you let the past dictate what you can accomplish in the future, you can be no more successful in the future than you have been in the past.

Have you ever done an IPO as CEO? If not, can you picture and believe that you could, or most certainly will? Or does your conscious ego take over and point out all the reasons why you can't ever do an IPO? Looking through the lens of the past, depending on wisdom and experience can minimize our belief system and affect what we can achieve in the future. To make this more frightening, we are not even aware we are doing it—framing the future only according to the past.

Let's check this line of thinking. Do you feel genuine excitement about your imminent success in the future? If not, then it may be that your past experiences are constraining your willingness to dream and find passion. We do this just to help avoid the potential pain of disappointment.

Let me tell you a story about a CEO, Javier. There are at least a dozen Javiers in my coaching past who exhibited the same emotion and behavior.

One morning Javier looked troubled. He reluctantly explained that the company had just lost a large client, but with the loss, this could be the perfect time to switch his product into a new market.

Sounds good, right? But I could smell his fear. He told me his product in this new market would do really well. But every time he brought up this pivot to his board, they shut him down. To make matters more complicated, this was not Javier's first rodeo. The last time Javier pushed a board to make a big change in a company, he was summarily fired and replaced by a new CEO. This situation felt like déjà vu. He was stuck between doing what he felt was right versus pleasing the board by delivering a message he knew they would accept. This was understandably very painful for Javier.

I asked him if there was any guarantee that, whatever decision he made, he wouldn't get fired again. Because, if he stayed with the same market space, one that he really didn't believe in, he was likely to fail. If he got the board's approval to move the company's focus to the new market, and it didn't work out well, he could fail.

I helped him understand that seeking safety was really dangerous. But more importantly, if he were to get fired, would he like it to be because he followed what he felt was best, or get fired because he capitulated to the board members' known desires? Which one would engender more regret?

Then I helped Javier see that if he pursued a path he really didn't believe in,

- He would lose his passion,
- He would lose his team, and
- He would most certainly lose his creativity and be really hard-pressed to authentically commit to a path he didn't believe in.

So even if staying the course was the right one, for Javier, it probably wouldn't work.

We reviewed how the past didn't have to equal the future, but it was difficult. Since his past experiences were so strong, they clouded his vision for the future. I reminded him that this was a new board, not the old one. I reminded him that this was a new play, in a new space, in a new time. Nothing from that past needed to influence today.

In the final summation of this story, the fear was too strong. Javier was too unwilling to find his courage and dare to dream to create his passion. He capitulated to his fear and didn't propose any change of direction to the board. The company struggled and ultimately faded into oblivion.

My bad. Maybe. My experience is that only about 30 percent of the CEOs in this place find their courage and become bold, decisive, and persuasive enough to follow their heart. Fear is strong, so don't let it get a foothold in your heart. Get out of the trance and notice what you are feeling. Be honest with yourself. The lens of the past is too easy to look through when viewing the future; it is part of the nature of the trance.

SNAP OUT OF THE TRANCE

Consider your entire past. See it for what it is: just your past. You learned from every experience, but those lessons don't need to be consciously reviewed. They already reside in your subconscious mind as wisdom. You can't get rid of them, and don't want to. They are part of your life.

But in the trance, we let our fears not only surface but allow them to direct our present and future words, actions, and decisions. And we rarely question that we indeed do have a choice. This is autopilot and the trance. If you notice that you have an emotion emerge in your heart, stop and look at the validity of the feeling. Question why you are feeling what you are feeling. Are you responding authentically in the moment? Is this the time and place to finally to break from the autopilot past? Yes, it is.

When subtle fear comes to the surface of your consciousness, you will often just stuff it back into the heavy backpack and add it to the emotional weight you already carry. It's easier to carry this burden than admit you ever were fearful. To be fearful is to admit you aren't that strong and independent. Instead, we spend time and energy writing stories to cope with all the fear that keeps popping up, and rationalizing why we can't do anything to change the trajectory.

With stories like, "It's Jeremy's fault. If he would only hit his sales numbers, then we would be okay," we make it Jeremy's fault, but we don't want to fire Jeremy because this is only the first quarter that we have missed our sales target. We never become aware of the trance that the story we wrote is essentially a story we created. Maybe it's just a bad quarter. Maybe our product line needs to be refreshed. Maybe Jeremy has no prospects in the pipeline, and it's a marketing problem. Maybe a new competitor is emerging and lowering the ASP for our competing product. But because we are living in a trance, feeling fear, and stuffing the feeling in our backpack, we write a story that is completely incorrect.

Oh, by the way, because we blamed Jeremy for missing the quarter, he blames people on his sales team because "feces flow downhill." Now the whole team is busy creating and telling stories about who is to blame for the miss. This process kills the sense of team, destroys creativity, and prevents us from finding the real truth of what happened. Left alone, these stories will annihilate passion, causing team members to spend more time refreshing their resumes than working to improve sales.

All this occurs because we fail to question our first feeling to any situation. We just go and act on our initial feeling, never questioning its source, and never recognizing that our current feeling may be driven by some wound in our past.

What actually happened is that we just missed our sales goal for this quarter. What does that mean? We missed our sales target for the quarter, period. Now in the space of no stories of why, and thus no blame, we now focus on what creative work can be done to increase sales. No one is to blame; we can just explore fresh ideas.

If we can recognize how the trance stuffs emotions down and causes us to automatically write stories (excuses), we can now understand we have a choice. We can take all our conversation, stories, and past and set them aside for a moment and stand in a new place of possibility. If there is no story about how Jeremy missed his quarterly sales goal, the miss can turn into the best news ever. Perhaps after pulling some data, the team tweaks the pricing as well as marketing focus, which results in doubling last year's sales.

You always have a choice. That choice is freedom. It's time you join the few in the world who are living out their lives on purpose. There is no gravy train, no free ride, and your ship is not coming in. But you can wake up from the trance and choose complete responsibility for everything in your life and live in the present moment. And in those moments, take bold action to create a life worth living. It takes nothing to sit on the sidelines to cover the story of your life like a reporter. It takes courage, intention, and commitment to continue to choose, in every moment, to be the author of your life. Come join the few.

TAKEAWAYS

- We all live in our trance. It is the autopilot that keeps us blind to choice.
- Our trance is like a momentum, a self-reinforcing power that keeps us thinking and acting the same, often ending up at the same old familiar location in our results.
- We get to begin living in this moment and quickly question our decisions, feelings, and actions to see if they are the result of acting on autopilot.
- Wake up and see every new event and situation as new. It's not a repeat of the past, even though the trance is screaming that it is.

19

THERE IS ONLY RIGHT HERE, RIGHT NOW

Hey wake up! The only moment you can live is this one right here, right now, as you complete reading this sentence. You can't relive yesterday and change anything. You can't even live the moments that will occur five minutes from now. Tomorrow is but a dream. You can't take tomorrow's actions today. You can't handle tomorrow's problems today. Here in this present moment you are alive, and you have choice.

Mindfulness is the consistent effort to bring your full attention to the present moment. During every moment of the average life, the mind is vacillating between a focus on the past and then the future. We conjure up a past failure that makes us face some guilt, or we write scary stories about how bad the future might be. Rarely are we living in and present to *this* moment. But living in the past, whether it's five minutes ago or twenty years ago, is mostly a waste. "The moving hand having writ, moves on."

We get bored thinking about the past, so we flip to the future. We worry about what is going to happen in the next five minutes or the next twenty years. While it is true that the first step in changing our futures is to dream about a brilliant one and be captured by our passion and plan, we must take bold action in the present moment toward our dreams.

The answer is to give up worrying.

That's easier said than done, I know. But I don't care if it is hard work. It's critically worthwhile work. Worrying about the future is a complete waste of time. We live in this present moment. This is the only moment where we have complete choice. This is the only moment where we can take action. But we fail to see how spending our time lost in the past, and worrying about the future, just causes more suffering to ourselves. When we live in this present moment, we find peace. Peace can render love for others. Peace and love for others create relationships.

Mindfulness is an incredibly powerful tool that is rarely deployed. Mindfulness is freedom of choice and freedom from self. Once we shake free of our stories about the past or future, we can dive into the present. This is why we spend so much time eliminating the baggage of the past, so it can lose its grip on our thinking.

What if you entered every new business meeting for the rest of your life, free from the judgments and predictions of outcome? What if you were completely present in every moment, focused on creating deep connection with everyone at the table? What kind of possibility and power could that create? What if there were no constraints on thinking and focus of any kind?

This is the possibility available to you when you are completely present in this moment, in relationships, making a powerful difference in others' lives. Is this possible? Of course, it is. Is it likely? Statistically not. It will take you consistently working on it for a while, until it becomes your new way of being.

What if you were called to the CEO's office, not being informed of the reason, and were able to just show up, be present in the moment, solid in your emotions, sitting down relaxed but with a passion in your eyes as you inquire: "You wanted to see me boss? How can I help you?"

How would you be perceived by the CEO? He or she would likely see you as being profoundly confident in yourself, which is really attractive. It would certainly look like no fear.

The CEO would think that this is the kind of person that they would want to give the most important roles and tasks to. The CEO wants to know that you got the ball, so they can rest easy with your department. Do you want to know what scares a CEO more than anything? A direct report who is scared. A scared direct report forces the CEO to ask penetrating questions, just to ally their own fears about your future performance. Yet, while you are in fear, you can't source a creative plan, so the CEO becomes even more concerned. Do you see how this can become a negative spiral? The CEO probably thinks, "This is more than they can handle, and it needs to be handled, so I better look for a replacement."

Life is intentionally created to be lived one moment at a time. It is our lack of attention to this moment that lets our mind aimlessly wander from the past to the future.

WHAT—ME WORRY?

Bring yourself to this present moment. In this present moment, what do you have to worry about? Really, in this present moment, what is there to worry about? The answer is nothing. There is nothing to worry about in this moment as you are reading this sentence. You might think, "If I think about later today, tomorrow, next week, or next month, I can come up with several things to worry about." Now that moment has passed, you are on to a new sentence to read, right here, right now. Now, in this new/next present moment, what is there to worry about? Still nothing?

Yes. If we learned the skill of mindfulness and took life like it was intended to be lived, in the moment, we would discover that we could enjoy a full and consistent life free from distraction, guilt, and fear. We could seize our power from past and future thinking. Bad things will occur in the future. But you will have plenty of time to feel badly about them then. When something bad happens, it will occur immediately, in the moment. No reason to worry about it now. You can't prepare for unexpected bad news. When the bad news comes, then you can get busy working the solution.

Bad things and good things are going to happen. We don't know which it will be or in what order, but we can learn to cross that bridge when we get to it. Life is dynamic, ever changing. By the time the next new event rolls into your life, you and your environment will have changed to something new. Your new options or new solutions will only be revealed at that new moment when the challenge presents itself.

The entire reason we regret the past and worry about the future is found in our insatiable desire for certainty about everything. We want to write stories about the past, filling in the blanks where there are no data. We want to write stories about the future, based on some veiled weather forecast of what might happen, so we think we can prepare. Often our preparedness is not based on all the facts; the issues will change and unfold differently than we expect, so the preparation is a ridiculous effort.

We so desperately want to know how everything is going to turn out because we crave certainty. But this is insane, because we know there is no certainty in life. Every day brings new challenges, opportunities, and solutions. There is only life, as it unfolds, moment by moment.

But we remember that the ego's job is to protect us from pain. The ego thinks that by worrying it can help you avoid pain. This is a lie. Worrying only makes situations worse. My ego would happily trade all the glory of success in every area of my life in exchange for safety and the avoidance of pain. The ego would love it if we lived our lives playing very small, but safe. The ego tricks us into believing that if we can predict the future, we can avoid or minimize the pain resulting from disappointment or heartache.

But the ego cannot predict the future—or any of the changes and new options that will surface. Plus, the ego does not have the interest or capacity to understand that worry creates suffering, which is what it is trying to prevent in the first place. It doesn't care. It just wants you to always avoid risks. Thank goodness there is another part of our brain that wants us to grow and succeed and live a large life.

In the space of living mindfully you get to notice important things like how you feel. Most of the time we gloss over what we are feeling and live inside the intellect. The great questions that a mindful person asks are these:

- What am I feeling, and what is the source of this feeling in this moment?
- Why is this feeling here?
- Is it a trigger from some past event?
- Is this feeling an intuition that something is not right, which is the effective working of wisdom? I should get busy checking this out further.
- Is this feeling the result of a story I have been writing for the last fifteen minutes (or fifteen years)?
- What is the black-and-white bare truth of the event I just witnessed? What are the facts without the story?

In this state of open and honest inquiry, I can see life much more like it really is, not just the way I have perceived it. In this space, of stark reality, I can make more powerful decisions. And I get to grow. Socrates suggested that "the unexamined life is not worth living." He wanted us to get in touch with what we feel and why.

A helpful tool for generating the skill of mindfulness is meditation. I am not an expert at this craft, but I personally see meditation as creating a space for God to talk to me. I pray, which is talking to him, and then meditate so he can whisper to me with an epiphany.

I admit that I have never been one who has heard audible words from God. But when I quiet my mind of all thought, especially after praying, something new comes to my mind. Sometimes it is guilt, or a memory of someone, or a vision of what I want to achieve. These messages are from the subconscious mind if you are not a believer, or promptings from God if you are. Either way, the thoughts, feelings, memories, or visions of the future during meditation are a prompting to dig when we leave the meditation exercise. They are an intuitive guidance. Each represent exactly what we get to take on next.

Intuition or epiphanies never emerge in the presence of a busy mind. They appear only when I quiet my conscious mind and allow the subconscious mind to speak. When I inquire to God or my subconscious mind, intuition speaks but only in a whisper. I have to be still to hear.

Have you ever misplaced your car keys? Okay, of course you have. But have you almost always found them? Of course, you have. When you have to leave for an important meeting and can't find your car keys, what do you do? Your conscious, analytical, logical mind takes over and says, "Let's retrace our steps this morning. In the last few hours where might I have set them down? Let's go look there."

Okay, that didn't work. "Where else did I go this morning? Oh, I went to the garage for a moment to get some more dog food. Maybe they are out there. Go look."

Nope, not there.

I call my wife and see if she happened to pick them up. All that accomplished was to bother her at work.

Finally exasperated, after fifteen minutes of retracing my steps, I give up and get a cup of coffee, pet the dog, and gaze out the window. Sitting there, with an empty and surrendered mind, it comes to me. My son borrowed the car last night, and when he came home, he dropped the car keys on the living room table. Lo and behold, there they are. My subconscious mind always knew where the keys were. I just had to find a way to shut down the conscious so the subconscious could speak.

Where do you get your most brilliant answers to problems and opportunities? Breakthrough epiphanies come when you are driving home, sitting on the toilet, or taking a shower, as I mentioned earlier.

During these times, your conscious mind rests because you are doing something that doesn't require thinking.

Mindfulness quiets the conscious mind. When you become present to this moment, the stories and worries get quieted also. In this quiet space the subconscious mind can render powerful solutions and answers. When you are free from worries about the future and guilt about the past, creativity and joy explode.

TAKEAWAYS

- Life occurs only in this present moment. Bring yourself to life, come home to the here and now.
- In this present moment, there is never anything to worry about.
- Worry and regret are the two worthless mental cancers that kill the possibility of you in the today.
- The subconscious mind already has all your answers. We just get to shut up the conscious stream of thought long enough to hear the answer.

20

"FREE AT LAST"

I borrowed a line from one of my heroes, Dr. Martin Luther King Jr., for the title of this chapter. If you are human, and if you have lived long enough to be hurt by others, then you are old enough to have experienced the resulting painful emotional wounds. You probably know the term—emotional baggage.

What is an emotional wound? It is a buried, painful emotion that emerges from time to time based on some past event.

Emotional baggage is collected when someone, probably many, have hurt you, and you have ignored or stuffed down the pain rather than sharing the pain with someone you trust, so you can process it, and let it go. Usually most people don't know how to process emotional wounds, so they take those resentments, those memories that make you wince, and try to stuff them into some box in the recesses of your mind. But that never works.

What you bury alive, stays alive. Maybe you have reconciled your logical mind to what happened and decided to let it go. But often this decision of letting go is nothing more than stuffing those wounds into a backpack, like they were rocks, and you wind up carrying them around with you for the rest of your life.

Over time, all these rocks add up and act as an anchor as you try to sail toward your dreams into a brilliant future of infinite possibility. Since we accumulate these rocks over a decade or several, we fail to notice the added cumulative weight. We usually never realize that we are carrying a burden. We often wonder why we have lost much of our passion. What has happened is your passion is buried under that pile of rocks.

We have no idea how the weight of this accumulated baggage impedes our progress toward a life we consider worth living. Because these emotional wounds are buried in our subconscious mind, we are often unaware of them. We have buried them so deeply that rarely do we ever feel them come to the surface.

When they do come up, we find ourselves reacting to a current circumstance that is larger than the actual current event calls for. So what do we do? We usually discount them and shove them back into the pandora's box in our subconscious mind where they have been kept.

What can be done? They can be removed, giving us the freedom to run toward a brighter future. The painful events of the past will always remain a memory, but they can become just a memory and only that—a benign memory having no impact on our current life.

I want you to become open to what most of us as humans are blind to seeing. The past often holds painful events, which in turn shape the context of how we view the world and our capacity to achieve a great life today. Some wounds are small, others devastating. The intensity of the wounds dictates what we do about them. A small wound may only require you to see it for what it is. Forgive yourself or others and make a heartfelt decision to let it go. A deep emotional wound may take more time and possibly require professional help.

Old unprocessed emotional wounds will impact your willingness to risk or be vulnerable. An emotional wound affects the way you look at the world, thus it can negatively influence your idea of what is possible. When emotional wounds rise to the surface, they can insulate us and prevent us from making human connections and relationships.

This protection does an efficient job of preventing others from hurting us again. You see, because we are still in pain, protection is still important—more so than is actually necessary. This cover does not stop the pain, but it serves as the lens through which we view others, and that lens can cause us to act less open, less positive, less vulnerable, and less able to risk and create human connections. And there we are, all the connections that make up a life worth living.

So what do we do about these old emotional wounds? Once we recognize and acknowledge them, the original events that caused the pain can be shared with a professional or a trusted friend. Shame cannot be addressed, because shame can only live in the dark and attack from behind. But guilt can be admitted and thus will evaporate through sharing. Forgiveness can only be chosen and realized by owning the event and then embracing it as a historical fact.

Finally, is it possible to carry emotional baggage and not be able to see it, or even recognize it piling around our feet? Absolutely.

Remember, when we are hurt, we blame others. This blaming stops healthy healing. If it is someone else's fault, we reason that there is nothing we can do about it.

Young children employ blame as a natural coping tool. But this practice of blaming early on only trains us how to stuff our hurts and pain through blame. If I can blame someone, then I don't have to process my pain, and I don't have to consider if I did anything to cause the problem. We insist it's not about us, it's about them and what they did.

I have an executive coaching client, Burton. He gave me permission to share his story, permission I sought because the story is so personal and moving.

The first time I met Burton, I spent the first fifteen minutes showing him that I was truly interested in him as a human being. He was not just another client. I wanted him to know that I deeply cared about him, his life, and his story.

After this get-to-know-you stage was complete, I opened our session with this: "In order for me to make our time together powerful for you, I need to know what you would like to accomplish with me. Give me my MBO (manage by objective) as it pertains to you. Give me a goal to accomplish. What would you like to achieve as a result of our working together? In other words, what is your main goal for your career life? Or even more simply put, what do you want?"

It usually helps to give clients an idea of what I mean, so I often say, "If through your performance and contribution to this team you achieve massive success, what would you do with the money you gained, which could be a few million dollars?"

Burton pondered for a moment and finally responded with an answer much like most of my first-meeting clients. "Gosh, Dan, I don't really know. I haven't really thought about it."

That in itself may not shock you, because if I asked you the same question, how would you respond? Do you know specifically what you would do with massive success?

I gave Burton a few more moments and prodded him again. What would be one thing he might do with the money that comes with success?

He looked up at me and said, "I would like to buy a house on the beach in Connecticut. That was where I was raised. And I have fond memories of my childhood there."

I responded, "Great. Tell me about the house. Paint a picture. A vision for your future must be something that has enough detail so that it can be described." What I was looking for was not just a logical and intellectual goal. I was looking for him to get in touch with the goal in an emotionally moving way. I want to see goosebumps as they get in touch with their dream.

I continued, "Describe the house. Is it pastel yellow with white window trim? Does it have a wrap-around porch? Can you see you and your wife on the porch with a cup of coffee watching the sun rise over the Atlantic, or do you see yourself with your wife walking on the beach looking back at the house?"

At this point, Burton paused and had a puzzled look on his face. I asked why he shut down.

After a couple of moments, he answered, "I don't know. I feel like I am stuck picturing the house."

I asked him where the stuck feeling resided in his body. He pointed to the bottom of his throat.

I said, "Let's forget about the house for a moment. Tell me about the lump in your throat. What's that about?"

At this point his lower lip began to quiver and he said, "Grandma."

I put the lump aside and asked him to tell me about Grandma. At this point tears were beginning to stream down his face, and he began to cry. He had found "it," and I let him cry. After about ten seconds watching him cry, I softly said, "This is perfect, you are doing great."

With his head in his hands, he let the crying loose. This emotional moment only lasted a few seconds before it subsided. I gave him another thirty seconds of silent support as he composed himself.

I asked him again, "Tell me about Grandma."

Burton told me he unconditionally loved his grandma, and she adored him. They were incredibly close. "When I was about six, I called Grandma on a Sunday like I always did. I wanted to tell her a joke and make her laugh. At the end of the joke she did indeed laugh, but then the laughter turned into a cough. Through the cough she said, 'Thank you, honey, but I have to go. I love you.'"

The next day, he learned when she hung up the phone she went to sit on the couch and had a massive heart attack and passed away.

When he finished telling me this story, he lost it again and began to cry. After a few more moments of crying, and the gentle pause of silence we created so he could be with this emotion, I said, "So you feel that you killed Grandma."

He gave no response.

Then I asked, "Do you believe in God? You know, the God of your understanding, not the God of some church, my church, or the neighbor's church. But a God of your understanding."

He said yes. I quoted the scripture, "It is appointed unto man once to die, and then the judgment." I said, "The key word here, Burton, is *appointed*."

I explained. "There is an appointment for us to die. That appointment is not set by us, it is set by God. Only he knows the moment. And we can't delay it one second, or speed it up. You did not kill Grandma with your joke, which made her laugh. It was her time. Period. When are you going to forgive yourself for something you didn't do?"

I told him that this was an emotional/spiritual wound, which cannot be healed with an intellectual solution. We can't fix a light socket with a pipe wrench. This emotional/spiritual wound can only be healed with an emotional/spiritual tool.

"I want to ask you to make a decision in your head and use the intention in your heart to forgive yourself for what you didn't do."

He looked at me and with his eyes he agreed. I told him to do it now. After a few moments, I said there is one more step. "I want you to bow your head in silence and pray to your God and ask him to heal that wound in your heart." He did.

After maybe a minute, he lifted his head. "I can't believe it. I have paid for hours and hours of counseling, and they have never discovered this issue. This is fantastic. I feel like a hundred-pound weight has been lifted off my heart and my shoulders. How did you do that? We have only been together for about forty minutes."

I told him, "I didn't. I am not that good. It was God."

I told Burton that I pray to my God before every coaching session. I ask God to help soften the heart of the person I am about to meet and to make me worthy for them to become vulnerable, so we can get some majestic work done. I ask God for direction of where the conversation should go. I ask him to bless my time with them. And I ask for healing to occur. It was God. He prompts me to see, without words, what I should pursue with my clients. He led me to leave the beach house topic and go with the lump in the throat. Then he led me to leave the lump and focus on Grandma.

By the end of the session, Burton couldn't wipe the smile from his face even if he tried. He was indeed free. Burton had lived with the incorrect guilt that he had killed his grandma. Because of his guilt and pain, he stuffed the event and the emotion. But what he buried alive, stayed alive. When he pulled the painful event to the surface, he could then see that there was no reason for guilt, so he could embrace the grief of the loss of his grandma.

A LIFE OF MEDIOCRITY?

All of us have emotional wounds. Some people carry devastating wounds that impact their future in significant ways. Many of us have smaller wounds that affect our lives in correspondingly small ways. But do you get the power in that sentence? Do you want to be negatively affected even in small ways? Gosh, in the Olympics, people win the gold medal in races by only 1/100th of a second. It is often the small things that take the edge off just enough that we end up losing the whole game.

Most people are really pretty good. They consistently come in second for a promotion. They almost got married to the one they loved. Their marriage is pretty good; in fact, it's good enough to keep them away from divorce. They were pretty good parents, raising their children with as much love as they had. Yet it wasn't enough, and those kids lacked the certainty of unconditional love and ended up using drugs or alcohol to help them cope.

So small emotional baggage takes the edge off our brilliance in life. Do you want a second-place life? Heck no.

Emotional wounds and the pain they cause make us focus on ourselves. Consider this: I am hurting and carrying emotional baggage, so because of the pain, I focus on me and how to make the subtle pain go away. When all that painful emotional baggage is gone, I tell myself, I'll begin to think about others.

So here is the problem I get to address as an executive coach. Most people have small emotional wounds. They aren't large enough to burst onto the stage of the conscious mind. But while these wounds lie in the subconscious, they not only fester but subtly run the show like a bad political advisor. This dynamic takes the edge off the executive's ability to love and connect with all those with whom they come in contact. This causes them to miss out on the win in every area of their life.

They say

- My marriage is good, not great.
- I like my job but can't say I love it.
- I'm good at what I do, but not great enough to move the needle in the organization.
- Compared to others, my life is on par.
- It's not bad, I am no worse off than my friends and colleagues.

That's not living large, that is not living to the fullest. Are they moving the trajectory of the company? Are they the author of a brilliant life? Or are they more or less a reporter covering the story of their life as if it's merely something to watch from afar?

Let's return to that backpack full of rocks that we carry.

You've got your own emotional baggage, and each of those small wounds adds in another rock. Every week another small rock is added to your pack. You barely feel the additional weight, because, after all, it's so tiny. Maybe an ounce.

After twenty years, the pack weighs 65 pounds. After forty years, the pack is 130 pounds.

How fast could you run carrying 65 pounds, much less 130? By the way, let's say that you start collecting emotional baggage (those rocks) when you are ten years old? You actually start earlier but let's keep it simple. This would mean that you are carrying 65 pounds of baggage by the time you are thirty. And 130 pounds by the time you are fifty.

But at the age of fifty you are in the prime of your earning years. You are at the pinnacle of wisdom coupled with energy. At this time, you could be bold, creative, passionate, loving, contributing, respected as a leader, and powerful. But as you look around, you see that most of us are not. We are bent over, slowing down, hauling our 130-pound packs. This problem drives me every day. This missed potential is a heart-breaking waste.

Since your emotional baggage is yours, you can choose to do something about it. You can forgive. You can choose to let it go. You can choose to seek professional counseling. You can choose to become vulnerable and share the original story behind the wound with a trusted friend. You can realize you are the only one who can own your pain and let it come to the surface to be experienced, so it can be addressed, so it can be processed and resolved, so you can start removing those rocks from your pack.

Your emotional wounds take the edge off your love, passion, and creativity. This baggage will cause you to come in second place for the rest of your life. Is this okay with you?

How do we release our emotional baggage, which makes us feel weighed down like an anchor? We need to dive into our pack and start pulling out the rocks, one at a time. Which means that we look at our life and begin to notice when we emotionally wince when a memory comes to our conscious awareness.

When we wince at something that happens to us today, it is often a stirring up of some event in our past. We take a moment and dig. When was the first time we felt this uncomfortable feeling? What event was attached to this feeling? When we do this work, we can often discover easily when it was, and what happened, and by whom.

This is the real first rock we get to pull out and examine. We look at this rock as just a black-and-white event. After we look at just the facts of what happened, we can then see where we have created stories about the event. It's in the stories where we suffer emotional pain, not usually the black-and-white event. We inspect them honestly and examine where maybe we were partly at fault for the negative event. If we find that we are to blame in some small part for the wound, we can then see that we added to the heft of the rock, and we then own it, which means we can now make amends.

If, when inspecting a rock, we see that we were not at fault at all, then we get to choose to embrace the event as something that can't be changed, so the only recourse is to forgive. One of the most powerful ways to drop emotional baggage is through forgiveness.

(I need to take a moment for a word of caution. If your wounds are severe such as witnessing a murder of a loved one, or rape or molestation, anything severe in nature, you will likely need the assistance of psychological/spiritual counseling with a professional. A few of these rocks can be so heavy, you can't lift them out of your backpack alone.)

Forgiving others and yourself is the best gift you can give yourself. What? Yes, forgiving others is a gift to you.

But you say, "They don't deserve to be forgiven for what they did." Oh, you didn't read the first sentence. It says that your forgiveness of them is something you do for *yourself*, not for them. Those who did you wrong may very well not deserve to be forgiven. So what? We still forgive so we can find freedom and peace for ourselves.

Bitterness and resentments from past wounds can pile up enormous crates of rocks. The more people you resent, the higher your walls of protection. The higher your walls, the less vulnerability you will be willing to offer. Yes, this brings you to a place where there are few people in your life. If you are attached to keeping your wounds, you will push away more and more people.

In extreme examples you become completely isolated and eventually become a bitter old man or woman who yells at the neighbor kids to stay off the lawn.

This is the end result of unresolved wounds and bitterness from unforgiveness. Forgiveness is nothing more than a choice followed immediately by an action. This is a choice you make not because you feel like it, but something you do despite how you feel. Wanting to forgive someone, or the feeling of forgiveness, usually comes only after you have forgiven them.

You can easily survive carrying your bag of rocks. You are perfectly able to get by, doing nothing about the past emotional wounds. Honestly, there is no compelling reason to take on this chapter at all, unless you want a brilliant, successful life, full of freedom, love, passion, and deep relationships, moving boldly and quickly toward success.

The key to removing your old emotional baggage can be best served by a professional, but if you can't or won't see one, at least share your pain with someone you deeply trust. Warning: If you have deep emotional wounds that you can't bring up to a friend, please seek out a licensed mental health counselor. You need not endure the pain of keeping those old wounds bound up inside you.

Get out of the dark recesses of your mind. Once you bring your old wounds to the light, they often just die. Shame is a great example of this. Guilt says I did something bad. Shame tries to tell us that we are bad. When the events that cause you to feel shame are shared, or brought into the light, they die. Often they turn into guilt, but we can deal with guilt. You can't deal with shame, because it demands secrecy.

TAKEAWAYS

- When we are wounded, we tend to stuff the emotional pain rather than processing it so we can let it go.
- This emotional baggage can be thought of as rocks that we carry around in our backpack.
- We collect more and more rocks over long periods of time and fail to notice the gradually increasing weight.

- When we notice how heavy our backpack has become, we can finally see the negative impact on our ability to move through life with a sense of freedom.
- It's usually not the black-and-white facts of the event that slow us down; it the pain that we have created as a story about what the event meant. And we have a choice to create a new and different story that carries no pain.
- Forgiveness is the final structural piece to this solution. Forgiveness of self and others lets the rocks fall out of our pack.
- Emotional baggage ultimately results in the creation of a bitter attitude, which leads to a life without human connection with others.

21

LEADERSHIP AND TOUGH LOVE

By now you may think that I just don't understand the real world. That all my talk of love and hugs can't possibly be effective in the real world. I get it.

There are those who were hurt and wrote stories of blame to cope with their pain or to make everyone else the enemy. They have repeated their internally written stories so many times it has molded their character and personality. They are entrenched in their bitterness and resentment and actually make it a point in their life to cause harm to others to justify and balance their pain. It's almost like people are saying subconsciously, "I am hurting somewhere deep inside, and someone is going to have to pay."

Fortunately, only about 5 percent of the people who have been referred to me as potential clients are stuck in this bitter loop. And I feel for them, but often I cannot help them. They are so vested in being right about everyone else being wrong, they can't hear me when I speak.

Question: How many executive coaches does it take to change a light bulb?
Answer: Just one. But the bulb has to be willing to change.

These 5 percent are not bad people, not at all. And I love them. I just get to love them from afar, until they are ready to surrender to a better way of thinking. Their issues are often not their fault. Maybe they were a kid caught in the crossfire of a parent's abuse, or they were born with a different physical appearance. But what they did, out of survival, was to create an internal story about the world. This story may have told them these messages:

- The world is not a safe place. Everyone is likely to hurt you or take advantage of you.
- People are jerks so don't become vulnerable and open yourself up to a relationship with them.
- Because I have doubled down on my learning to make up for my flaws, I am going to be smarter than them, and so I will show the world that they are stupid.
- I never get what I want or what is fair. Everyone else gets acknowledgment, but not me.
- I know what I say hurts people, but they are so dumb, they deserve it.
- I don't care if I am liked. I don't care what others think. I do my job, and I will call them out to do theirs. If they don't like it, they can come tell me to my face, if they have the courage to face me.

When they are on our team, what do we do with these poor souls? We love them. We lovingly tell them that their actions, behaviors, and attitude are not acceptable here, because the team is more important than any single individual. We tell them that they need to change if they are willing, and that we will support them in that change. We also tell them that they have X days to transform, or they will be let go. And we follow through on that commitment.

If you love your team, really love them, then you will be willing to become uncomfortable while making them uncomfortable. Do you have difficult conversations with your children when necessary? Of course you do—because you love them. A true portrayal of love is being willing to have difficult conversations. The key is to have them from a place of love.

It saddens me deeply that most leaders avoid conflict. They wait until they get angry enough to reprimand a direct report, and then out of that anger, the direct report takes it personally. The reprimand is no longer about the action or the behavior—the issue has become personal. In these cases, the direct report can't hear the reprimand, they just get defensive and throw blame. And I can't blame them for doing that.

Here is what a reprimanding conversation might sound like when it's done in love:

"Paul, thanks for coming to my office. Hey, I heard you told Sally that she does crummy work and ought to be fired. Is anything like that true?"

(Paul makes excuses and rationalizations.)

"Well, Paul, I have found that companies win because of the orchestration of a team, not superstar individuals. I place incredible importance on team, in fact more so than I place on any individual. You should know that I take personal responsibility for this situation between you and Sally. You are on my team, so everything you say, do, and act is my responsibility. I can't go to the CEO and tell him that we missed our target goal because Paul can't get along with Sally. I have to tell the CEO that the miss was my fault, because everything that goes on in my team is my responsibility."

"Look, Paul, we pride ourselves in making great hires. I don't believe that we blew it by hiring you. You are really good in these three areas (explain). But this behavior is completely

unacceptable. Paul, what's going on in your heart to have this situation exist? I will come alongside you and support you in having whatever is broken fixed. But we don't go to blame, and we don't throw other team members under the bus. What do you suggest we do when it comes to you?"

(Paul points a finger of blame about Sally again and doesn't get it.)

"Paul, I can't fix Sally here in this meeting. Because she's not here, you are. I am meeting with you about what you wrote, said, and did. Because I am responsible for the team, more than the individuals, I am going to have to remove you from the team if this doesn't change. And I hate having to do that, but it is my responsibility to create and lead a team that works together to win. I am paid to build and lead a team that works well together, at all cost. One last time, Paul. What can I do to support a fix in this situation as it pertains to you, and what's going on inside of you?"

In the cases that don't improve with a loving reprimand, and you have to let them go, do it from the place of love. Since you've had this conversation three times now with Paul, and you have given him ample notice, and HR feels that you have built your case, and the liability of a wrongful termination case is mitigated, it's time to act.

What is important to realize is that you are the leader. You are responsible. You are in charge. Stay in charge at all cost. When you confront a bitter and stubborn direct report, see it for what it is—a test of wills—and you have to win, or the inmates will run the asylum.

If a direct report verbally pulls a knife on you, you pull a gun. If they pull a gun, you pull a canon. If they pull a canon, you pull a howitzer. If they pull out a howitzer, you go nuclear with a firing. But we can do this always coming from love.

In addition, we don't want to create deep emotional wounds from a firing as the former employee now needs to quickly secure another job to provide for their family. We realize that they are going to have to tell their significant other that they were fired today. We want the least damage done to the person being fired for all the reasons I have stated. So what does a "loving firing" look like?

PULL OUT THE BIG GUNS

Before I begin, I need to tell you a true story I have done with clients maybe five times. I am not suggesting that it will work for you. The culture of our country has changed a great deal in the last ten years. But it will give you a great example of pulling out the big guns when necessary. Please read the disclaimer at the end of the story. So don't get sideways as you read.

Scott, the CEO, called me for help. He told me that he has two really talented superstars, each skilled at what they do, each critical to the company. But they are fighting. "It's never been good between these two VPs, but now it is getting worse."

The relationship between these two, we will call them Phil and Geno, has deteriorated to the point that Phil and Geno are having public arguments, and the arguments are becoming personal. They are building camps of support. They are copying too many of the wrong people on email chains to build their own personal case as to how right they are and how wrong the other guy is. The conflict has now reached the point that people are joining one camp or the other. There is no collaboration between the two teams, and there is no creativity happening due to the toxic environment and fear.

When I met with Scott. I summarized the situation as he described it and then confirmed, "Do you agree that this situation has to be resolved at all cost, and quickly?" Scott agreed.

I told Scott that I could solve the conflict in one day. Yes, one day. But I needed just one thing from him as the CEO. Scott agreed to do whatever was necessary.

I told Scott that I wanted to meet with one of the two VPs at 10:00 the next morning. We would be meeting until noon.

Next, I wanted to meet with the other VP from noon until 2:00.

After that I would meet with both of them from 2:00 until 4:00, and for the next hour, all four of us would meet. I asked Scott that no one else was to know the schedule.

The one thing I needed from Scott was the hardest. I stated the terms. "Because the problem is now affecting the whole organization, and that we both agree that it must end, and end now, I have to know if you are willing to fire either Phil or Geno at 5:00 p.m. tomorrow. I don't know either one of them, so I have no bias as to which one should go, so you have tonight to figure that out. But I just need to know that you are willing to fire one of them, if we can't fix this tomorrow. Do you agree?"

Scott looked shocked, but since the whole company was at stake because of the possible destruction of the sense of team, he agreed.

Next morning at 10:00 I met with Phil. During the first five minutes, I told him about me and the work I do so he knew who was sitting in front of him. Then I told him that I had been brought in to resolve the conflict between Geno and him.

We were into the meeting six or seven minutes when I asked this: "Phil, tell me all about the nature of the conflict between you and Geno."

He went off. He told me how often Geno was wrong, and all the bad things Geno had done. I only asked clarifying questions to keep him going. At the end I told him how much I appreciated everything he had told me. I made sure he knew that he had been completely heard and understood. (This is critical.) I noticed that much of Phil's built-up steam had been released after sharing with a person who aggressively listened.

At noon I meet with Geno. I had the exact meeting with Geno as I did with Phil. Now both of them felt that they had been completely heard and understood. Their story had mattered to someone, without being judged. Much of the visceral anger had dissipated.

At 2:00 I meet with both Phil and Geno.

Here is exactly what I said: "I want to thank each of you for meeting with me and telling me everything on your heart about the conflict you have been experiencing with each other. I have met with both of you separately and completely heard everything you have said. I never intended to take sides, and I haven't. I don't know the long history or complexity of the full story between you. I have only heard what you individually feel. I don't know who is right and who is wrong, and, frankly, I don't care. What I do care about is that the conflict ends—today and forever."

I continued, "You may be thinking that is a tall order, but it's not really. That said, the solution to the conflict is up to the two of you, not me. I don't have a bag of glitter and hearts to sprinkle over you to fix this. But you do need to know that I have faced this a few times, and I have come to know that unresolved conflict is not like wine. It does not get better with age. And the conflict between the two of you is now affecting the whole team.

"I asked Scott, your CEO, yesterday morning if he understands the gravity of not fixing this problem by end of business today. Scott understands the grave nature of this conflict and has agreed to fire one of you at five o'clock today if I can't solve the problem. Scott agreed to do so. I will not weigh in on who should be fired. Gosh, I only have two hours with each of you, so I don't know who should go. I leave that up to Scott.

"So we have two hours to end this conflict forever. Then we meet with Scott, all of us together."

I asked them the ultimate question: "So what do you guys want to talk about for the next hour and fifty-five minutes?"

I DO NOT SPEAK ANOTHER WORD.

At this moment if I say one word, the exercise is destroyed. It usually takes from three to five minutes for one of them to speak. I move my eye contact from one to the other with a calm sense of love on my face knowing perfectly well they are both frantically visualizing what they will say at 6:00 p.m. when their spouse asks about their day.

How will it sound to explain they were just fired because they couldn't get along with that VP, you know, "the one I've been complaining about over the last three months?"

The absurdity of having to tell your spouse that you lost your job because "you couldn't play well with others in the workplace sandbox," not to mention the financial stress that would bring, is just not acceptable. It is worth giving them both a moment to ponder the outcome of their attitudes.

Finally, Phil spoke. "Well I guess it's not all Geno's fault. I could have handled the meeting back in September better. I was just thinking that Geno didn't understand the pain he was causing my team when he said X."

After a moment or two Geno said, "I didn't have to go to the CEO and tell him how wrong Phil was with his decision to do Y."

Now that ownership of fault was coming to light, the other person was not wanting to be left with guilt when they saw the other basically apologize for their action. I sat silently not saying a word while they owned their own part in the conflict.

Finally, one of them continued. "My mom died four months ago, and I have really been upset."

The other said, "Gosh I am sorry to hear that. I didn't know."

They continued to talk to each other, they have to, because I remained silent. About ten minutes before our two-hour meeting was up, they have reconciled.

I finally spoke. "Well it's about time for all of us to go see the CEO. Are we good? Is the conflict dead—forever?"

In every instance so far, they agreed.

I told them as a coach I often see people say the right things, and I believe what they say and that they mean it. But I always ask for tangible evidence that the conflict is over for good.

I asked them to stand up and give each other a hug. Fortunately, up until now this work has been between two men. I tell them that I will only know for sure that they have reconciled when I see evidence of it. And I am only comfortable telling the CEO that the conflict is over, when I feel it truly is.

"I don't mean a bro-hug with a pat on the back. I mean a real Leo Buscaglia hug. Are you guys willing?"

And I sat there and shut up again. About a minute later, after a little more chatting, they stood and hugged.

At five o'clock, we three marched to Scott's office. I announced the VPs had ended their conflict. I asked each of them to share what they each did and what they regret. "Own your own stuff. Don't speak about the other guy."

They did.

Then I told Phil and Geno they needed to convince the CEO that the conflict was really over. "The only way I know how to do this is for you two to stand up and hug." Scott's eyes grew wider as the two men hugged once again.

Now I told them they have one more task to cement their new relationship. It is a requirement of mine to make sure I have done my job. I told them the story about how many men in World War II created lifelong friendships from just spending one night in a foxhole.

"You see, a foxhole is dug for protection and security. Shrapnel and gunfire can't get you when you are below ground level. Here is where I believe the saying 'I have your back' comes from. Picture two guys sitting in a foxhole. The best thing to do is to put your backs up against each other. This allows each man to visually cover a 180-degree view. Your warm back up against another person's warm back keeps you warmer than leaning up against the cold soil of the foxhole. Note that there is human touch going on here, which releases dopamine and creates connection in a profound way.

"During the entire night, neither can sleep, so they whisper to each other. 'Hey what's your name? Where are you from? Are you married? What did you do before the war? Do you like the Yankees or Red Sox?

Have you ever gone bass fishing?' They tell stories of their childhood and share dreams of their life after the war. They connect in relationship, which eases the fear of war. Inside the intense environment of heightened emotions, they bond."

Back to Phil and Geno. I told them I needed their commitment to go on a business trip together within the week. As the VP of engineering and the VP of marketing or sales, they could visit a client. There was one rule for the trip. Since they are both men (or they are both women), they are to drive to the airport together. They are to sit next to each other on the plane. They are to travel to the client's office in the same rental car. And they are to have every meal together.

I asked them for their commitment. I waited until they agreed. I didn't care if they had to rearrange their schedules. I didn't care about the cost. The whole future of the company could depend on this next week.

[Disclaimer: I am sixty-five years old, I have done this exercise only with men who are over forty years old. In my experience, the awareness of PC problems were not in our conscious thought. So as a broad warning, I wouldn't do this today, in this culture, if I were you. The legal liability would be too high for you. Because of my reputation and experience, I would deploy the exercise again but with some deep understanding of the individuals and I would proceed with caution. Having to put this disclaimer in here saddens me. Because my heart is pure, and the intent is only good. But this is the world we live in. You, the reader, get to sense your own PC discernment and find the way that is comfortable for you to show love. I can't tell you what is right for you.]

As the leader, it is important to get really clear about your intention. Is the idea of team in the company, which is essentially a group of individuals, the most important element? If you see that the culture, creativity, boldness, joy, alignment, or passion of the company is being harmed by one individual, you can't keep them. Some exceptional employees are just too expensive to keep.

An interesting fact: Of the thousands of executives I have coached, not one has ever admitted to firing someone too quickly. They either fired the employee at the right time or, more often than not, waited way too long to take action.

Do everything from a place of love, even the hard stuff. Be honest with yourself as to what the company needs you to do. Don't rationalize. In this instance of a firing, can you see how important it is for you to be clean of emotional baggage so you can stay grounded in the midst of conflict?

TAKEAWAYS

- A small number of people have been so emotionally damaged, they have just become bitter to everyone, about everything.
- Reprimand a direct report out of love so they can hear the feedback without getting defensive.
- For the purpose of maintaining the chain of command, you never let a direct report hold you hostage. Lovingly, you always pull out a bigger stick if necessary.
- Tap into the power of a foxhole to mend a conflict.

22

IF YOU CHASE IT, IT RUNS

Here is one of life's great paradoxes. Often what we desperately seek and chase actually runs from us. If you are committed to being in a relationship with a prospective mate, and you pursue them with dogged commitment, it can look like stalking. If you are committed to being rich, and with single focus to go about making money, it looks like greed and desperation, and no one will want to be on your team.

Let's pick a few simple goals as examples to illuminate this principle. By the way, these principles apply to almost everything you pursue.

You may be thinking:

- I want a loving spouse.
- I want friends who are loyal and trustworthy.
- I want to be recognized and appreciated for the work I do.
- I want a new car. The new car requires a promotion.

There is nothing intrinsically wrong with these wishes, but they do represent a self-centered focus. When you come from I want and I need, you will find it more difficult to achieve your dreams.

But you say, "If I don't go for what I want, then I can never get what I want. I have to look out for me; no one else will."

That's a lie. When you get into relationships with people and really care about them, they will love you and want to see that you win too. Charity and love are contagious. By helping others, you also win.

The best example of this is in sales. When you walk through the front door of a new prospect with the whole idea of closing a sale, you are focused on what you want. The buyer can read this a mile away. They see salespeople all day long, so they are subconsciously good at reading people. But if you were to walk in with the intention of helping the prospect, even if it doesn't include a sale for you, they can read that as well.

What if you were to suggest an alternative solution to their problem that might involve doing something other than buy your product, and you made a phone call to help set that up? Often, the prospect will ask you to quote pricing on other products you sell to meet other needs they have. Be a selfless contribution to the prospect, while looking for the ways that your product and pricing might just be exactly what they really need.

You no doubt have had direct experience with a self-centered person. All they can talk about is what they want, how they deserve it, and how others are not helping them achieve their dreams. Do you want to have coffee again with someone who only talks about themselves? Alone, these people have no one to advocate for them. They become isolated. They are not getting the promotion because no one on the team wants to spend time with them. Trust me, their boss knows who is liked on the team and who is not.

I want a loving spouse. There is nothing wrong with wanting to be loved, but with an intense focus on finding a loving spouse, you must see that you are seeking what you want, not what you can give. Your prospective partner will see that you are solely focused on you and your needs, and that has them put up their walls of defense against you. From their perspective, you could start to look like a series of obligations and duties they are expected to perform to make you happy. That is not love.

I want a new car, which would require a promotion at work in order to afford the car I want. Again, nothing wrong with a new car. But what happens if you approach your boss with a promotion request for the hidden reason that you want a new car? A promotion to a leadership position will likely include an increase in the number of direct reports, but you are focused on your own wants and needs, not being in service to a greater number of people.

During the conversation you didn't speak about wanting to make a bigger difference to the organization, you talked about how you deserve the job based on what you have previously accomplished. A promotion is not a reward for past work. A promotion is a signal of confidence that you want and can perform well at the next higher rank of responsibility.

Your boss will likely see you as self-centered, which in turn would translate into poor leadership attitude. Who in their right mind would promote someone with a selfish attitude?

I want friends who are loyal and trustworthy. So right off the bat you want your friends to meet your needs. Because you have probably been hurt before by a friend who was not loyal or trustworthy, your ego will remind you to stand back and wait to see if a new acquaintance is worthy. Want a loyal and trustworthy friend? Be a loyal and trustworthy friend to others first, with no condition that they have to respond in kind. Your new loyal and trustworthy friend will emerge.

I want to be recognized and appreciated for the work I do. You can see a person who is seeking applause from a mile away. You can sense their desperate need for appreciation. They want the glory and the credit. And that's the last thing you want to give them. As much as you may deserve credit, the seeking of applause, and jockeying for position, will cause you to fall into last place. Try to gather up all the credit and you'll be left with none.

COMMITTED BUT NOT ATTACHED

On the other hand, let's say you are still committed to having a loving spouse, car, promotion, loyal friends, recognition, and appreciation. But in this instance, you have decided to let go of your attachment to having to have those things. They are a desire, but no longer a need. You would like to see them come to you, but you have chosen to focus on others first. In fact, you have made others your main goal. You and your wants and needs are a distant second. You still want your dreams to come true, and you are committed to doing what you can to create them in your life, but they take second place to putting others first.

Here is what this new attitude would look like.

I want a loving spouse. You decide to show up to the world like a loving spouse. You exhibit to the world, as a model, what it is you are seeking for yourself. Because you love your spouse and realize that they probably want the same things in the relationship you do, to be loved, appreciated, accepted for who they are, and supported with kindness and affection, you become the most loving spouse in the world.

When you do this, 90 percent of the time your spouse will become incredibly grateful for who you are and how you show up for them. They will experience you as the one person in the world who completely loves them and is in their corner, and you want them to win. When you give, they will almost always respond with deep love and appreciation for you, over time.

If you are already in a committed relationship that you want to improve, your new attitude and action will take time, maybe lots of it, to show results. This is because you have a history of not being this way. Your significant other is going to want to watch and see if this is real. It takes time. But is it worth it? Heck yes. What else do you have to do with your time? Get a divorce attorney? This is how you get a loving spouse: You become one first.

"Oh, but what if the other person just becomes a taker and never gives back?" That could happen, and now you know that this spouse is not right for you. You have given them all your love, unselfishly, and it didn't make a difference. At least you know that if both of you are takers, you have no chance at getting a loving spouse. Plus it is actually more satisfying to love unconditionally even if you do not receive love back than to be resentful and wounded for not being loved enough.

I want a new car, which would require a promotion. While I am committed to doing the work that is necessary to earn a new car, I will not let it become an idol or an obsession. This way I can get off the obsession and focus on how to make my boss more successful. If I am willing to make a selfless contribution to my boss and others, I will be loved and respected. I don't mean I become a doormat. If I am in a one-sided relationship where I give and give and nothing ever comes back, I can choose to leave my job, or a friend. I have boundaries that I set so I will not be used by others. But I focus on supporting, helping, being involved with my team, and providing authentic guidance for what will be most beneficial to others.

When I do this, everyone on my team will recommend that I be promoted because they would love to work for me, and everyone, by my contributions, will see that I deserve the promotion.

This is how you get a promotion, which comes with a pay increase, which makes the new car possible.

I want friends who are loyal and trustworthy. Vulnerability, passion, and loyalty are contagious. Be trustworthy to your friends and they will respect you. In addition, they will mirror your actions. The best way to get loyal and trustworthy friends is to be a loyal and trustworthy friend yourself. Now there are times that loyalty and trustworthiness will not be reciprocated. Okay, then we gently move that person out of our inner circle of trust. We never dislike them; we just learn to guard our heart from them and continue to seek those who are worthy.

I want to be recognized and appreciated for the work I do. The best way to get recognition is to not seek it. When people really want the limelight, the people around them are really resistant to giving it.

Attention seekers are insecure. Instead, give the glory away to others. A great leader always takes the blame when things go wrong and gives away all the credit to the team when things go right.

I know many humble and enlightened CEOs who get it. When things go wrong, they take all the blame. "Gosh, the buck does indeed stop here."

But when things go right and victory is theirs, they give all the credit away. "Thank all of you for the applause, but I have to tell you that it is my team back home that deserves all the credit. I am constantly amazed at their creativity and commitment to excellence. I am in awe how much they truly love our customers. It is indeed an honor to work alongside them."

When the employees back home hear this kind of public acknowledgment during a speech or during a press interview, it cements their loyalty and encourages them to work even harder on behalf of the company.

Here is the bonus for this kind of selfless humility: Other great employee candidates hear this kind of praise for the employees from the boss, and think, "Man, I would love to work for a person like that. He or she is such a great CEO." This is how to attract talent.

You can't give credit and kudos away fast enough because the glory keeps coming back: "Best place to work in Cincinnati" award. Front-page picture of you on the trade journal with this headline: "Fastest Growing Company in Our Sector." And in the interview you say, "Gosh I am so blessed to work with such great people. They are the ones who deserve all the credit. Let me tell you about just one of them, Marilyn. She led her team to..." There is so much more power in true humility than people understand.

So here is the paradox in a nutshell.

If you want to be happy, don't seek to be happy. It will run from you. Seek to make others happy, and you will discover happiness in yourself from the response of others.

If you seek money, it tends to run from you. Seek instead to offer help and value to your prospects, customers, peers, direct reports, and boss. If you seek to give to others, they in turn will make it a point to make sure you win too. If you happen to be in a cutthroat company where this will never work, what do you suspect my advice to you would be? Move to a company that will reward this kind of behavior. To stay there, you will have to become cutthroat yourself to survive. Do you want to lose yourself, to keep your job?

One of the hardest things to do is to want something, and then let go of your attachment to having it. Experiment. Next week, get in touch with what you want, let your passion swell up, and dream of having whatever you envision as if it were already here, then commit to forgetting all about yourself and make every action you take be an unselfish gift to others.

Think only of them, not you. See how much you can give of yourself at every opportunity. Open every door for somebody. Smile at every person serving you behind a counter and ask them about their day. Look people in the eye and tell them how much you appreciate who they are and what they do. Give love. Seek nothing. See what happens. It will blow your mind. It is likely you will not get your goals accomplished in one week, but you will move toward getting them, and you will find peace, joy, and happiness in the meantime.

MY NEW FRIEND RAY

Let me show you how this works.

I was flying back from Orlando where I attended a conference in 2019. On the flight back there were two legs to the trip. From Orlando to Denver, then from Denver to Sacramento. On the leg from Denver, I was assigned a center seat in a row of three.

My first thought was about whether I was going to play a turf war over the armrest, or if I would be a loving, giving person and fold both arms in and just be giving to others.

My second thought was that the person who booked my flight, two months earlier, could have chosen either a window seat or an aisle seat. They must not care about my comfort.

My third thought was to stop the previous two thoughts. I saw that I had a choice in my stories and quickly chose to create a different one.

I decided that I would do whatever I could to make the person in the aisle seat next to me comfortable. It was near the end of boarding when a nicely dressed 6 foot 2 black man came down the aisle and put his luggage in the overhead bin above me. I reached over and unfolded the two seat belt straps so when he sat down, he wouldn't have to dig them out from under his butt.

He thanked me. Now I wanted to use some discernment here. This man may want to be left alone in the quiet, or he may want to meet me and talk.

So I proceeded carefully. "Flying out or flying home?"

He told me that he was flying into Sacramento to meet his wife and mother, and that they were all going to Napa to meet his sister. It felt like he was open to talking so I introduced myself and he introduced himself, Ray. He lived in Houston and was a recently retired attorney.

We then engaged in a lively conversation, and I shared my favorite story about Leo Buscaglia and the hug that changed my life. The flight went by in a flash.

When we landed, Ray rose and stepped back away from the exit door. I looked up thinking he was just being polite and letting me exit first. As I got up, he said, "I just want a hug."

Wow. So here are two guys, an old white guy and an aging black guy, who have known each other an hour and a half, standing blocking the aisle and all the anxious passengers for a full three seconds. Really hugging, no bro-pat on the back going on. On the way out of the plane, he asked if we could exchange contact info. I said with enthusiasm, "Of course, I would love that."

See what can be created out of nothing when I forget me and focus on being there for others? My flight went by like a flash. I made a new friend. I was moved, inspired, and transformed when I left the flight, and I got a story to add to a book.

A word of caution here. You want to make sure in your honest heart that you don't become a doormat or a servant to others. There is such a thing as codependence where everything you do or say is all about pleasing others. This kind of giving never gets rewarded. There are those in the world who are takers. They like it when you put them first, but you'll find that you don't experience any joy in the relationship.

If you are giving to others and you find no joy in your efforts, it may be time to lovingly separate yourself from them. Relationships, good ones, are win/win experiences. If you feel that you give and give and get nothing back, stop giving and move on. If you don't, you will become their victim, and this will engender heavy resentment. Listen to your heart. It knows if you should keep giving or walk away.

When I truly focus all my attention on others, all of my wildest dreams come true. There is tremendous joy that comes from giving to a grateful recipient. It takes time to melt the heart of others, so don't expect appreciation right away. Don't continue to give yourself away when you feel the relationship is not worth the effort. Everything you seek will come when you give it all away. And I know that makes no logical sense. But do it anyway.

TAKEAWAYS

- Selfishness and self-seeking keep people and the universe from giving you what you want.
- When you give to others, they want to make sure you get what you want.

23

RELATIONSHIPS: THEY ARE YOUR WHOLE LIFE

I am going to make a bold statement. I invite you to examine it closely and see if it is indeed true. After some contemplation, I hope to make it true for you if it is not already.

Relationships. They are your life, your whole life. There is no life or living without relationships. You don't have a life without relationships. Relationships are the beginning, middle, and end of the experience we call life. Let me prove my point.

You tell me, "Not necessarily true for me. I love fishing: My life is fishing." Okay, I have an offer to make to you:

Option 1: I will send you on a fishing trip. I will pay for it. I am not referring to a fishing tournament. A tournament would include other people, and that would be about relationships. I am referring to your love of fishing on any given Saturday. I will send you to my favorite fishing spot and you will catch twelve huge fish.

But you have to go alone. You will drive there alone, launch your boat by yourself, then drive out to the spot I tell you and fish all day by yourself. The place I am sending you is secret. You will not see another soul all day. You can stop anytime you want and eat the lunch I have prepared for you. You will eat alone. You can't take a cell phone with you, because you could use it to talk to people or search social media. You can't do that because that would be about people, not fishing.

You will finish the day and drive home alone with your huge catch of twelve big fish. You get to clean them alone and put them in the freezer. Without your phone you can't take a selfie of you and the fish to show anyone, because that would be about a relationship, and you can't call anyone and tell them about your bounty for the same reason. This is just about "my life is fishing." Do you want to go?

Option 2: I will set up a fishing trip for you and your three best friends in the world. Magically it could even be someone you loved but who has passed away. Maybe it's your favorite uncle or your dad. You will spend the entire day with the three most beloved people in your entire life just fishing, laughing, and recounting stories of your past together. Before you leave you don't know you will get skunked. But no one will catch a single fish.

Which do you choose? Option 1 or option 2?

We could play the same game with golf. People say, "I live to play golf. Golf is my life." Really? Well I have clout at your local country club. I have just arranged a membership for you to golf at the finest country club in your area. I just bought and paid for your membership.

But here's the catch. You can't ever speak to anyone in the clubhouse or on the course. I have made a special arrangement with the golf pro for you to go out every Saturday morning with a tee time of 8:00 a.m. But you will always go out as a single. The rule is that you can't chat with anyone on the course. No one. And if you play a scratch game of golf, you can't tell anyone. You can't post your score either. You are here to golf, because golf is your life, not relationships or people.

Do you take me up on my offer?

Someone might say, "I like working alone in my shop making things, like a custom rocking chair from scratch." Woodworking is my life. Great. I have just bought you a complete woodworking shop. But here is the catch. I am giving you the shop because you like to build things with wood. Woodworking is your life.

But you can't tell anyone about what you make. If someone sees something you made yourself, and complements you on how fabulous it is, you must lie and say, "I have no idea who made that." You can never point to anything you made and show it off to your spouse or friends, because that would mean that your woodworking was in some way related to people, not just the joy of working with wood. No one will ever acknowledge you for your craftsmanship. But I will keep you supplied with the finest tools and the rarest of wood materials.

Do you want my free shop and all the free exotic woods you can use?

The next person says, "I love writing alone with my cup of coffee and my laptop." Great. I just gave you enough money to completely retire. You don't have to do anything but write. However, no one will ever read a word you have written. I heard you. You said your life is about writing, but you didn't mention that it was important for others to read what you write. If you wrote for others, then it would be about relationships.

Everything we do is ultimately about relationships. Relationships are the most important connections in our life. You may even come to embrace relationships like I do—nothing else matters here on earth without relationships.

HOW ARE YOU IN THE RELATIONSHIP DEPARTMENT?

Let's look at the quality of your relationships:

- How well do you get along with your husband or wife or partner?
- How is your relationship with your kids?
- How about your extended family? All is well there?
- How about the relationship with your boss?
- How about your work colleagues? Doing good there?
- How about the people who are your direct reports?
- How about your neighbors?

- How well do you get along with your friends and acquaintances?
- How about your relationship with the people in your state when you travel?
- How are you at getting along in relationships with the other citizens of our nation?

Since relationships are our life, not just a priority or a goal, we begin to see our whole life as relationships. Only when we see their importance can we discover a new and profound desire to create good ones.

Satellites prove my point that we are all about relationships. Remember seeing a satellite image of the United States at night. Remember how there are bright spots in LA, New York, Boston, Dallas, Chicago, and Seattle. Why? Because a concentration of light comes from concentrated areas of human population. But look at all the dark areas in between. Some people call these the flyover states.

I did a quick analysis of the population of the US and calculated it against all the acres of tillable land. It turns out that if we just spread out, create some elbow room, and live with a little space around us, each American family could have their own 4.26 acres of tillable land. So why don't we just spread out? Why do we want to live on top of each other? It is because we are genetically driven to be in relationship with people. We always have, and always will have, a deeply driven desire to be in community.

Even in the early ages of our existence we lived in small villages or communities. According to archeologists, village populations were about 150 people. There is not only safety in numbers, but mates as well. The village offers the opportunity to specialize: One group farms, another hunts, another protects the village. Our distant ancestors could have formed a spear, gone to a village, found a mate, then left and created a home in a cave, with a fire, away from the village. But they didn't. They stayed in the village. Even our ancestors validate that we are genetically driven to be in close proximity to others so as to be in relationship.

We need to be in relationship with other people; we really don't have a choice in the matter.

And we are in relationships with everyone we meet. Some may be extremely shallow, like the woman at the gas station you opened the door for, while some may be mission critical to your life, like a spouse.

You may be saying, "I am not in relationship with my dad. We haven't talked for ten years. I hate him, and he hates me."

Well here's a news flash. You are indeed in a relationship with him. It's just an extremely poor one without communication. Having poor feelings toward a person proves that you are in relationship with them. If we didn't feel anything toward another person, never saw them, or never spoke to them, this is the only time we are not in relationship. When we embrace that we *are* in relationship to everyone we know, we are confronted with the responsibility of choice.

Since I am in relationship, what am I going to do with it? If I can see that I am in a troubled relationship with someone, and have ill feelings toward them, I must realize that I am the one carrying the pain. If that is the case, then I get to choose to heal that bad relationship so I can feel emotionally free. The only other choice is pain.

Now there are those people in the world that we honestly feel want to harm us, so we stay clear of them. But most people in your life do not fall into this category.

Since we are in relationships, and we are genetically driven to be in them, we now get to decide what kinds of relationships we want. It becomes a choice outside of the stories that we tell ourselves. If we look at our relationships and feel we are a victim, then we are left with no choices or power to create the relationship into something new. But when we see relationships as a genetically driven need in our life, and we see that some of them are broken, we can then take responsibility to heal them.

Since relationships are my life, when I mend, create, or build better relationships, I am actually improving my life. So giving to others, and pouring into relationship building, is an incredibly rewarding and healthy selfish thing to do. You focus on others to get what you want. Great relationships.

So how great do you want your life to be? Which can be translated as, how many great relationships do you want?

I hope you are saying, "I want a great life, so I want to build a ton of great relationships."

Relationships, shallow and short, or deep and sustained, I want to build them all with everyone I meet, everywhere, all the time.

I told you a story about Ray, the man on the plane who hugged me goodbye. Let me tell you about the middle of our conversation that morning.

After about twenty minutes of conversation, I said that I wanted to tell him something that would be hard for him to understand, but that I would be willing to explain myself immediately. He said okay.

Dan: "I love you Ray, because I truly know you."

Ray, with a puzzled look: "Okaaaayyyy."

Dan: "Do you pee light yellow?"

Ray: "Yes."

Dan: "Do you bleed red?"

Ray: "Yes."

Dan: "Have you ever felt betrayed by someone close to you?"

Ray: "Yeah—"

Dan: "Me too. Wow it hurts. I know exactly what that feels like. Have you ever triumphed over a difficult task and felt overwhelmed with excitement, like pumping your fist in the air and beating the steering wheel as you yelled YES?"

Ray: "Yeah, I have."

Dan: "Have you ever fallen in love, with profound infatuation, like you would give your whole heart to that person, and do anything for them?"

Ray: "Oh, yes, I've felt that."

Dan: "Me too. I know exactly what that feels like as well. You know it strikes me that we have felt the same emotions. I know exactly how you have felt. I know what it feels like to feel like you have felt. Being a white man, I have never felt just one thing—discrimination due to the color of my skin. But I would love to try to understand what that is like, so I could grow in my understanding of you. Being a black man, you could help me understand that one feeling. But everything else in your life is the exact same as mine. I may not know all your stories, but I do know the most important thing about you. I know how you have felt, and I have felt all those things too.

"So I know you. Because I know you, I have compassion for you. This compassion makes me love you. Now, I get to be in relationship with you to hear the stories that have made you feel the way you have felt."

He hugged me because of our connection, not to be polite, not to be correct, but to connect.

What new or deeper relationship can you create today with your boss, peers, direct reports, prospects, customers, board members, strategic partners, extended family, neighbors, community, or maybe just some guy on a plane?

Does this kind of connection happen all the time? Maybe it could. Maybe not. But I get to use discernment to see if it's possible with the very next person I encounter.

How great do you want your life to be? You will experience limitless possibilities once you are rid of your past emotional baggage. You will be free from self so you can focus on others from a place in your heart of compassionate love.

Think of the ripple effect of any one of these brilliant relationship opportunities. A concept first proposed in the 1990s by British anthropologist Robin Dunbar, Dunbar's number suggests a limit on the number of people you can maintain a stable social relationship with. He found a correlation between primate brain size and average social group size. By using the average human brain size and extrapolating from the results of primates, he proposed that humans can comfortably maintain only 150 stable relationships. Dunbar explained it informally as "the number of people you would not feel embarrassed about joining uninvited for a drink if you happened to bump into them in a bar."

Starting with Dunbar's number of 150, let's say you have a positive impact on 150 people who have a positive impact on their 150. We are talking about just one ripple.

The number of people affected by you in the course of just one month, through one ripple, would be 22,500. Now let's say that your impact was so profound that it moved those 22,500 people to impact their social circle of 150 people just one more time.

With just two ripples, you would have impacted 3,375,000 people.

You can indeed change the world in short order, if you influence your social circle with peace and love so powerfully that it makes two ripples. The third ripple would impact 506,250,000 people.

Since relationships are your life, what do you want to see when you look back on your life? Who will be standing around your deathbed? How many will attend your funeral? Family and friends or the hired help?

Who are you? Really. And what are you going to do about it? You are only going to travel this planet one time. Are you wasting your calling and potential? Your calling or destiny is where your greatest joy meets the world's greatest need. What is that for you? It's worth considering, it's worth planning out.

We are inescapably driven to love and be accepted and be loved and accepted by others. We can't change that genetic drive. Since we can't escape that we want to be loved and accepted by others, and to love them right back, we might as well embrace getting really good at it.

TAKEAWAYS

- If we are really honest, everything we want in life includes people.
- We are genetically wired to be with people, and you can't change that.

24

LOVE—
THE HOLY GRAIL

If relationships are your life, and thus critically important to you, then what is the core catalyst in creating and empowering these relationships? It is love. Period. Love is what we all seek.

Because of the pain many have experienced in relationship with others in the past, they have often buried their desire to be loved. But the desire still remains. Many people have arrived at a place where they don't really feel worthy to be loved but can't admit it, which is why we see so many who, it seems, simply can't receive our love. If we tell someone how much we appreciate their dress or suit, they often say, "Oh I had that for some time. It wasn't that expensive." Give someone a genuine compliment, and just watch many of them squirm. They don't know how to receive a genuine compliment. If they could receive love, they would simply say, "Well thank you."

We have built walls of protection around our hearts, which have insulated us from human connection. Many people can't even see their hidden desire to love and be loved. And they certainly won't admit it. I have heard people say, "I don't need anyone. I love my alone time." This is denial. While alone time can be healthy and gratifying, it should be enjoyed in short intervals.

Love is the complete acceptance, appreciation, and desire for companionship even in light of who you are at your worst, and who they are at their worst. We are all human. We have brokenness that we deal with or bury. We are flawed human beings, in a flawed world, wanting love from flawed people. What do we expect? But the desire to love and be loved sticks to our hearts like glue. We can't escape this truth. Many people try to find escape in drugs, alcohol, shopping, pornography, social media, food, materialism, or any one of over 200 12-step–related *dis*-eases.

The tragedy of this predicament is that we will always want to be loved, but our defenses are so powerful, and our desire for safety and protection is so strong, most people feel stuck between wanting to be loved and the desire for protecting our hearts, which keep us from being vulnerable. This can seem like a challenge that is greater than our ability to conquer. Personally, in the grand scheme of things in the world we live in, I believe it may be. For me, personally, I get to/have to turn to the God of my understanding to change my heart, as the result of my request for this in prayer.

How about your children? I have heard psychologists say, "Regardless of what happens in your child's life, they can handle it if they know they are truly loved."

How about extended family? Lots of people have said there is nothing more important than family. We are stuck with each other. We can never leave family without tremendous pain. Love is the elixir that heals, bonds, and binds a family together, especially in the midst of a "hot mess."

The family unit is a powerful force when it comes to the ability to endure hardship. We are supposed to be able to turn to family when our life crashes. But the reason why family can be such trouble is that we deeply care about them. Because of this deep desire and past vulnerability, they can hurt us more than anyone else. It reveals the deep need for love and acceptance in the family unit more than anywhere else.

How about friends? Now these are the people we get to choose. Most people will say they have a friend who is closer than a brother.

Your closest friends know everything about you, usually more than your immediate family. There is something magical about knowing there is a person who loves you so unconditionally that they will never leave you, especially when you realize that they could. The love of a dear friend is not an obligation, it is a choice. And that makes this kind of love really special.

How about your boss? He or she doesn't wake up in the morning thinking, "I can't wait till I get to work and make life miserable for my team." Heck no. But they may wake up feeling miserable, and as a result they arrive at work and accidentally make your life miserable. The driving force behind their crummy behavior is their emotional baggage, burden, responsibilities, and pressures. But in some small way, they hold your career in their hands.

Wouldn't it make sense to find a way to know them well enough to love them, to understand what makes them tick? It would be such a salve on their pain for them to see that they are loved by you, especially when they are a prickly pear cactus. One of the biggest reasons why they may be a jerk is because they have been hurt in the past instead of loved. So their defenses went up long ago, and with that, they are not very approachable. I am not saying you should kiss up. That's repulsive. Nor am I saying that you should become a doormat to anyone's abuse.

But you can offer a kind word. You can thank them when you are genuinely grateful for something they have done. You can inquire as to how they are doing, even though they will likely never answer. It is the authentic interest in them that can change everything. How do you think they would respond if they knew they had a team behind them that really cared about them as a human being, not just as their leader? Over time, pure love melts the hardest heart.

How about your peers? Instead of trying to show each other up, what if you loved each other and supported your shared success? What if everyone on the team felt that there was unconditional support when they hit the wall?

While with peers, it's important to become personal friends, but not so much with direct reports or your boss. When it comes to your relationship with authority, personal separation and respect maintain a smooth chain of command. In the battle for success, you and your peers are comrades in arms. Your bond with peers can be one of the more rewarding relationships you can have. There need be no power struggle. And since you spend a minimum of eight hours at work, you essentially spend half your waking life with these people. You probably spend more waking hours with your work colleagues than you do with your family. Coworkers are a huge part of your daily life.

How about your direct reports? They don't care how much you know, until they know how much you care. How great is it to work for someone you trust who will always be in your corner and is working as hard as you are to win? How great to know they are willing to go the extra mile for you to succeed?

When you authentically love your direct reports, they will love you back. As their leader you are directly responsible for empowering them so they can succeed. Here is the problem. Most managers think they can't be open, take risks, and be vulnerable to their direct reports, because the employees will likely try to turn it into some kind of friendship for a promotion or a hall pass in the case of a mistake. This need not be so. You can love your direct reports and hold your boundaries and standards all at the same time.

Do you realize that what you do, how you act, what you feel, and how you show it will have a profound impact on an entire family for two generations to come? How great would it be if you could be around to hear one of your direct reports at age eighty tell a story about their best boss, and their best boss was you?

How about where you live? Do you love your neighbors? I have lived in a neighborhood where there were regular block parties on the weekend. My neighbors became my friends. We loved each other. They lived only a few hundred feet away from me, but they were closer to my heart than family. It was so cool to know that my neighbors were looking out for me, my family, and my property.

How about the guy who sits next to you on the plane, a complete stranger? Like the story of my new friend Ray. Love makes an airplane flight go by like it was minutes, not hours.

I want to be clear here. Love is an emotion, and it's a decision. It's not just random acts of kindness or a gentle response to a harsh comment. Love is not just turning the other cheek. These are the fruit of the emotion of love. Many people try to do or say loving things. They want to behave lovingly and do nice things for others. But that is not enough.

Love takes work on your part, work to rid yourself of past emotional baggage to end selfishness of attitude. It takes a decision, then internal work, to become authentically loving. But without the emotion of true love in your heart, good deeds amount to little. To make a difference, do everything with love.

Humans are incredibly astute at reading people. We have decades of experience in reading the intentions of others. I have told clients hundreds of times that nothing sounds like the truth, like the truth. We like to think we can fool people with our agenda and our mask. The truth is, we rarely fool anyone. They may not know your agenda, but they can feel when it's not genuine, and this makes them hesitate to come along with you no matter what your proposed journey is. It is really safe for me to tell you that whatever is in your heart is seen by everyone.

I know you probably wanted me to give you a checklist of things to do to be a great leader and be loved. I can't. There are no powerful techniques that work. There are only ways to be.

Love is unconditional. Love is only love when it is given expecting nothing in return. When you love others, you are free from resentments, bitterness, expectations, disappointment, and judgment. It is in these times that my heart is full, I enjoy peace, and I know my life is making a difference in this world. I wouldn't trade that feeling for anything in the world.

TAKEAWAYS

- Acceptance is the first step to love.
- We get to face our fear of rejection in order to find deeper love.
- Coming from a place of love is hard work. The work is putting others first.

25

AUTHENTICITY AND BOLDNESS

I deeply want you to live a full life, whole and complete. I want you to feel joy, peace, and contentment. I want you to be the author of your life, play on the field, and not sit in the bleachers. I want you to take action in your life, starting right now, to create a life that you say is worth living.

This will take you becoming deeply honest, starting with yourself. It will take becoming aware of your thoughts, your feelings, and your fabricated stories about life, and having the courage to ask if these stories are really serving you. With this awareness coupled with self-honesty, you can then find the power to choose to make changes in your life as its author. Now you have a choice. Choose carefully. This may be the last time in your life that you are confronted with who you really are and who you really want to be.

In order to create a brilliant life, search through the memories of your past and let go of resentments and bitterness. Heal old wounds. This work is going to require you to be vulnerable and recognize the real truth of your life. It is critical that you be completely honest with yourself. This process will create some emotional pain as you recognize what you thought were immutable truths, but were instead simply fabrications and self-created stories.

Whether you are a CEO of an international conglomerate or a Silicon Valley start-up or someone who aspires to become a leader in any endeavor, you will do this because you finally now realize that people can discern and fully see the authentic truth in people. They can see through the mask of overcompensation, denial, and rationalizations, which make us form the masks that we wear. And when you reveal who you are and how you are feeling in front of others, they will be moved, inspired, and transformed. You will see that vulnerability is indeed contagious. When you become authentic and vulnerably share yourself with others, they will also become vulnerable and share their truth with you.

When you do this work, you will discover a new and profound peace within yourself. This peace will become a clean and solid foundation upon which you will stand as you face life. When you come to this place of being peaceful and solid, you become unshakable; you become your real self. And inside, you are a magnificent creation, just as you are.

AUTHENTICITY

I had a chance to coach a brilliant CEO. His company was in the top fifty high-tech companies in the world. We will call him Jason. When I met with him, I discovered a most powerful principle at work: Be honest when you make a mistake.

Jason told me, "I want to create an organization where honesty can flourish and is the accepted norm and the hallmark of everything we do. Look, we all make mistakes. It is in the concealment of mistakes where we waste vast amounts of time and money and miss opportunities due to the wasted time going down rat holes.

"So if someone in our company makes a mistake, or an error in judgment, and it comes to their awareness that it is a mistake, we ask that they admit the error and stop pursuing that path, immediately. We need to feel safe enough to call out our personal mistakes so the company can stop spending money and manpower on an errant path. We need to quickly turn away from that path and take a new one. Our time to market is too important to waste following what we know isn't right."

Of course, in principle, Jason's approach makes perfect sense, but most of us are reluctant to implement such a policy because of the fear of being blamed.

As a CEO, Jason knows this and seeks ways to model this behavior. He also realizes that everything filters down from the top.

A few years ago, he held an all-hands meeting and told the team, "You know that large initiative we have been working on, code-named Hercules? We just spent one and a half years and $14 million on it. I killed it today. It became clear that the product idea was not right and was not going to work. I am sorry, because Hercules was my idea."

Wow. Jason just made it completely okay to try, fail, and call yourself out as the culprit of the idea. His own actions modeled the company culture. Jason's company is phenomenally successful, and you'd know the name of the company right off if I told you. I believe their massive success is in large part because of Jason and his personal commitment to honesty, humility, and focusing on success. He has no interest in being right.

Jason is an example of being authentic. He calls out his faults because he loves success and he loves his team. He is willing to bear the cost of pride and fame for the sake of seeing his team win. And here is the oxymoron: When he admitted that Hercules was his mistake, respect for him in the company soared.

As we have covered, we always write stories in our head. Most stories are not the black-and-white truth; they are some form of a slightly twisted story that has some foundation of truth. We write stories so we can make sense of the world we live in. We are constantly pretending not to know something so we can avoid pain and make our world a little more convenient. We say and write stories to project what we want others to see.

Most of the time, most of us are not completely authentic. Authenticity comes with a cost. We may not get the response we want when we plainly speak our truth. But the high price of authenticity also has an incredibly higher payoff. When we are authentic, people get the real facts and nuances of what we think, so we cut to the chase and make better decisions. When we are authentic, we move the conversation powerfully forward. The depth of understanding that comes from authenticity creates real connection with others, as in "I know where he stands," as opposed to "I am not sure where he's coming from."

When we are authentic and honest, we avoid wasting time on blame. Responsibility is owned by someone right out front, enabling the team to quickly move past the problem and focus on the solution.

BOLDNESS

Boldness moves people and mountains. People step aside and give way when you are bold. But there are two kinds of boldness: bully boldness and real and powerful boldness.

Bully boldness is cheap and detrimental to progress. This is the braggadocio form of boldness. It is manipulative and controlling. Bullies hold on to their power through intimidation. Arrogant bullies destroy team communication and kill any desire for the team to follow them.

This second form of boldness is mighty and powerful. It is boldness with humility. This kind of boldness allows people to see that you are solid in your stand on a matter, that you are energized and committed. This form of boldness is internally focused. It is not about controlling others and what they think or do. When you are in the presence of this kind of boldness, you do not feel pressured at all by the bold person. You are instead drawn and inspired to follow them because of the trust that is ignited in you by *their* strong belief.

TAKEAWAYS

- Become honest with yourself, before you try to be honest with others.
- Authenticity is the magic of connection, progress, and team.
- Cop to your mistakes to save wasted expense, build teams, and ignite corporate honesty.
- Be bold with humility.

26

CHARITY: LOVE IN ACTION

When I write about charity, I am not referring to money. Charity is something much more.

Charity is giving of yourself, selflessly to others. Here is where I get to wrap all this material up into one profoundly powerful virtue and claim where everything of value is found. It is the root of all relationships and leadership. It is love.

Remember the dental clinic in Mexico? The need for dental services was so great that even as we built up the clinic, my friend Don was practicing dentistry. While I punched holes to install the water supply lines, a few feet away Don was working on a small girl's abscessed tooth. I asked him if he wanted me to continue with my work.

He said, "We have to. There is a line of people outside that we have to see while we are doing construction."

I glanced over at the little girl in the chair as I was reaching for a small jackhammer. The poor thing looked miserable, all swollen and in pain.

Later that night all of the volunteers piled into our single house for the night. I answered a knock at the door. There stood a young girl holding a tray of food covered with a white linen cloth. I couldn't understand all that she was saying, so I called Don over to talk to her.

Don spoke with her for a few moments and then slowly closed the door. As Don turned around with the tray of food in his arms, tears streamed down his face.

"I know this family. We pulled a badly abscessed tooth from her sister today."

I said, "Yes, I remember her. But what's the problem?"

He was by now finding it difficult to speak. "This food represents all the food her family has in the house. She just gave us all their food. If I turned it down, it would be a terrible insult."

I will tell you that night, every one of us bowed our heads for grace.

That's love.

Love was the driving force behind Dr. Martin Luther King Jr. He didn't come from judgment or bitterness. It was love that drove him to speak at the Lincoln Memorial when he said, "I have a dream that my four little children will one day live in a nation where they will not be judged by the color of their skin, but by the content of their character." It was love that drove his intention for the peaceful marches.

It was love that drove Mother Teresa to save hundreds of people, many of them children, from the ravages of disease and starvation in Calcutta and elsewhere.

It was love for his people that drove Mahatma Gandhi to use nonviolent resistance to promote civil rights in India.

It was love that made Abraham Lincoln take a stand for racial equality. He didn't want to go to war; it deeply troubled him. But it was love for all the people in the country that resulted in the Emancipation Proclamation.

It was love that made Sir Nicholas Winton risk his own life to smuggle hundreds of Jewish children from Czechoslovakia and thus sparing them from the Nazi concentration camps.

There are millions upon millions of stories of sacrificial love. What is your story? If you don't yet have a story, then, if not you, who? Only you can make your unique contribution. If not now, then when? Why will tomorrow be any better? Start right now. Find one place that you can make a difference and start there. I think of this planet like a campsite. When I leave this campsite, I want to leave it a little better than how I found it.

True love inspires, moves, and transforms us into becoming better human beings. Love lasts.

The most richly rewarding part of my work is not seeing the success that my clients create, which is the primary stated purpose of my work. No, it's experiencing the human connection between me and my clients; then it's experiencing the deep relationship created between the leadership and their teams. It is when I hear a client say, "I took what you said about business and used it at home, and it worked really great."

Love, connection, loyalty, and friendships last forever. The glory is revisited anew in the stories we remember. Life is rich because of our stories—both successes and failures. One of the biggest benefits of aging is how our collection of stories has grown. Our stories become a repertoire of tools that can help others in their search for real meaning.

I wish you well on your journey. I love you, because I know you. I can't wait for the possibility of meeting you face-to-face and give you a big Leo Buscaglia hug. I want to hear your stories of pain and triumph. I want to learn about that glorious moment that you dumped that last rock from your backpack and, unencumbered, flew into your own fabulous future.

Be rich in all areas of your life, my dear friend.

TAKEAWAYS

- Love is only experienced when it is shared.
- Love only has power when it is revealed in action.

I HATE TO LEAVE YOU

Please know that, as I was writing this book, I was writing to you personally. Yes, you, reading this sentence right now. I can't picture your face, but I know your heart. I may not know your story, but my heart is moved toward you right now because I love you. I love you because I know you. I know how you have felt, and because I have felt the same emotions as you, I have compassion for you. And it's out of this compassion that I find love for you.

That realization of shared emotions makes us have something quite powerful in common. Even though my writing and your reading is occurring at different times, I am still very much with you.

I truly love you. I already miss you as I tell my fingers to stop writing. I hope to bump into you somewhere along the trail. I want to give you a hug. You really do mean the world to me.

If you would like to contact me, please do so. I would love to hear from you. Here is my contact information:

Dan Foxx
Unlock Your Leadership
www.UnlockYourLeadership.com
DanFoxx@UnlockYourLeadership.com

ACKNOWLEDGMENTS

I want to thank a few of the many people I am grateful for.

God. I wouldn't be alive without him. The gifts I have are from him. The love I feel in my heart he has given me.

Kathleen, my wife. The love of my life. The kindest and most supportive person I have ever met. She says yes to all my crazy ideas. She teaches me every day how to love others.

Of course, Dr. Leo Buscaglia, for showing me what unconditional love and acceptance was in a parking lot in Lake Tahoe. Leo passed away just a few short months after our chance meeting in Tahoe, but those ten minutes with him changed my life. Thanks, Leo, I will never be the same.

I am grateful to all my clients. They gave me a platform to do this work, for teaching me so much about myself, and for giving me money to put food on the table through my coaching practice.

Mike Riley, for being there in my darkest moment. Dave Zabrowski, for stretching out a hand when I was ready to stand back up. Gina, for believing in me when everyone else was rolling their eyes. Cavett Robert, who taught me that helping just a few was more than enough. Eric

Jensen, who went the extra mile to be there when I needed it most. Dave Mullan, for showing me the way out of the darkness to freedom.

Mom and Dad for their love early on and for showing me how to embrace hard work.

America, for giving me the freedom to write what I want without fear.

ABOUT THE AUTHOR

Dan Foxx has been an Executive Coach to CEOs, VPs, and Director-level executives for the past twenty-two years, working with over 400 CEOs and 4,000 VPs. He began his work as an Executive Coach in 1997 and has worked with such household-name companies as SanDisk, JDSU, and SAP.

Early in his career, he was a salesman, a VP of Sales, VP of Marketing, and President of a manufacturing corporation. Dan started and built a full-service advertising agency in the late 1970s and worked with over 300 clients.

Dan is a sought-after keynote speaker. He speaks to executive leadership groups, employee groups, and sales associates with topics such as relationships, leadership, passion, the power of commitment, and corporate strategy. His most recent speech in 2019 was for management-level executives at Calvin Klein in Amsterdam. His TEDxChelmsford Talk titled "The Hidden Truth about Human Connection" is available on YouTube.

His work with clients has been featured in *Inc* magazine as far back as the year 2000.

Dan and his wife, Kathleen, live in Grass Valley, California.

Made in the USA
Las Vegas, NV
13 January 2022